ARCHIMEDES

and the Door of Science

by JEANNE BENDICK

Pictures by the author

Bethlehem Books • Ignatius Press

Bathgate, N.D.   San Francisco

Originally published by
Franklin Watts, Inc., 1962

First Bethlehem Books edition, September 1995

Bethlehem Books • Ignatius Press
10194 Garfield Street South
Bathgate, ND 58216
www.bethlehembooks.com
1-800-757-6831
Printed in the United States on acid free paper

Cover art by Jeanne Bendick
Cover design by Davin Carlson

Publisher's Cataloging in Publication

Bendick, Jeanne.
   Archimedes and the door of science / Jeanne Bendick. —
[Rev. ed.]. — Bathgate, ND : Bethlehem Books, 1995.
   p. cm.
   Slightly rev. from 1962 ed.
   Includes index.
   SUMMARY: Biography of one of the most important
scientists of Ancient Greece, and an explanation of his
contributions to physics, astronomy, and mathematics.
   ISBN: 978-1-883937-12-6

   1. Archimedes — Juvenile literature   I. Title
QA29.A7B46 1995   LCCN: 95–78182
510'.92   QBI95–20368
Manufactured by Thomson-Shore, Dexter, MI (USA); RMA579LS388, January 2012

Contents

Introduction

Archimedes and the Door of Science is a wonderful book and an outstanding teaching tool. Jeanne Bendick has succeeded in creating a book that is interesting in itself, as well as helpful in any history or science curriculum.

Archimedes was a most remarkable ancient Greek. Our own culture is deeply indebted to the Greek civilization in which he lived. For example, many of our best ideas about education come from the Greek system of education, which is engagingly discussed in the early chapters of this book. The single most important idea about education, in fact, comes from Archimedes and those like him. Their attitude toward truth, the idea that truth is important for its own sake, not for its practical applications, is of enormous importance.

Additionally, the scientific and mathematical ideas of Archimedes, presented here in a way that is both accessible and stimulating (not always an easy marriage!), have formed and informed western thought on those subjects. Archimedes discovered and developed the principles of the sciences of mechanics and hydrostatics. He discovered the principles of buoyancy and specific gravity, as well as the laws of the lever and the pulley. He figured out how to measure a circle, and gave to mathematicians a way of working. There are those who say that he was the greatest mathematician ever.

The author's presentation of the particular ideas and contributions of Archimedes, combined with the underlying attitudes and certain characteristics of the world he lived in, make a kind of whole that is singularly engaging. *Archimedes and the Door of Science,* in story form, allows one to assimilate, painlessly, many facts about Greek culture and the way of life of its citizens. One also begins to understand the Greek attitude toward knowledge.

The best way to learn theoretical ideas at a young age is to see them embodied in particular people. It is not enough to say to a child, "The truth is an end in itself." Standard textbooks often fail this way. They tell the facts, but they don't bring those ideas to life. Even the most interesting ideas may seem dull and boring if they are presented too abstractly. In contrast, *Archimedes and Door of Science,* by showing how exciting Archimedes found ideas, and exploring those ideas, allows the reader to experience some of the excitement for himself. In keeping with its title, this book makes a door through which a young reader can enter.

The author's integration of Archimedes' scientific ideas and his personal history, along with the views which he, and others of his culture, held about education grant a further boon. It gives the reader an experience not unlike the education discussed in this book, where every discipline is seen to be a part ofthe truth, not to be understood in isolation from the other disciplines; an important concept and a valuable experience.

Laura M. Berquist
Ojai, California
August, 1995

ARCHIMEDES AND THE DOOR OF SCIENCE

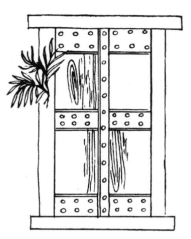

(1)

Who Was Archimedes?

ARCHIMEDES was a citizen of Greece. He was born in 287 B.C. in a city called Syracuse, on the island of Sicily.

When Archimedes was born, an olive branch was hung on the doorpost of the house to announce to all of Syracuse that Phidias the astronomer had a son. A slave dipped the baby in warm water and oil and then wrapped him in a woolen band, from his neck to his feet, like an Indian papoose.

The birth of Archimedes was celebrated by two family festivals. When he was five days old, his nurse, carrying the tightly wrapped baby in her arms, ran round the circular hearth in the main living room of the house, with all the other members of the household, both the family and the slaves, running behind her. This ceremony put the baby forever under the care and protection of the family gods.

The tenth day after he was born was Archimedes' name day. Phidias had a party for all the family and their friends. In front of all the guests he solemnly promised to bring up his son and to educate him as a citizen of Greece. Then he gave the baby his name — Archimedes.

It was just a single name, without a first or last one.

2

Maybe Archimedes was named after his grandfather, or a friend of the family, or a god. Much thought went into giving the baby a name, which was carefully chosen to bring him luck. Then the guests piled their presents near the swinging cradle, a sacrifice was offered to the gods, and finally a great feast was served.

The family gods must have looked kindly on the baby Archimedes, and his name must have been well chosen, for he grew up to be one of the greatest scientists the world has ever had.

Most of the things *you* know about science would have dazzled and bewildered him. But many of the things you know about science *began* with Archimedes.

What was so unusual about a man who spent almost his whole life on one small island, more than two thousand years ago?

Many things about Archimedes were unusual. His mind was never still, but was always searching for something that could be added to the sum of things that were known in the world. No fact was unimportant; no problem was dull. Archimedes worked not only in his mind, but he also performed scientific experiments to gain knowledge and prove his ideas.

Many of his ideas and discoveries were new. They were not based on things that other people before him had found out.

Imagine what this means.

Nowadays we do not have to think about most things *from the beginning*, because we have the knowledge of all the things that men have learned over thousands of years.

The great mathematicians of modern times have the knowledge and the proofs of thousands of other mathematicians to help them. The greatest scientific discoveries are based on things other scientists have learned, bit by bit.

A famous scientist once said that he was able to see so far because he stood on the shoulders of giants. Archimedes was one of the giants. He was one of the first.

The scientists who came after him had more and

more to work with. Archimedes had only the principles — the basic ideas — of the great mathematics teacher, Euclid, and these ideas —

that a straight line is the shortest distance between two points,

and that the next shortest distance is a shallow curve,

and that each deeper curve is longer.

That's not much! But the mind of Archimedes — that curious, logical, wonderful, exploring mind — made up for the things people before him had not found out.

Archimedes began the science of mechanics, which deals with the actions of forces on things —

solid things, like stones and people,

liquid things, like water,

gases, like air or clouds.

5

He began the science of hydrostatics, which deals with the pressure of liquids.

He discovered the laws of the lever and pulleys, which led to machines that could move heavy loads, or increase speeds, or change directions.

He discovered the principle of buoyancy, which tells us why some things float and some things sink and some things rise into the air.

He discovered the principle of specific gravity, which is one of the basic scientific tests of all the elements.

An element is a basic substance. There are no combinations of substances in an element. Gold is an element, and so is silver, and so is lead.

The gas, hydrogen, is an element, and so is oxygen. But if you combine them together you get water, which is not an element, but a compound.

Archimedes discovered that every element, and even every combination of elements, has a different density, or weight for its size — and that this is a good way to tell one substance from another, even if they look alike. The density of any substance, compared with the density of an equal amount of water, is its *specific gravity*.

He invented the Archimedean screw, a device that is still used to drain or irrigate fields and load grain and run high-speed machines.

He invented a kind of astronomical machine that

showed eclipses of the sun and moon. He estimated the length of the year, and the distances to the five planets that were known to the ancient world.

For three years his war machines defended the city of Syracuse against a great Roman fleet and army. But although he was a great inventor he considered inventing an amusement, and mathematics his real work.

Archimedes wrote brilliantly on almost every mathematical subject except algebra, which was unknown to the Greeks. (You can't have algebra without the idea of zero, and no one thought of zero until hundreds of years after Archimedes lived.) Some of Archimedes' mathematical theories were so complicated that even today they can be understood only by experts.

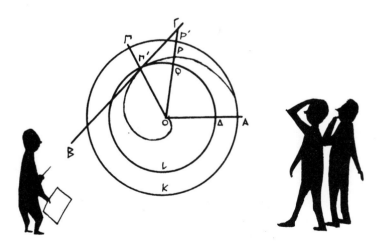

He was the first to show that numbers unimaginably big, bigger than all the things there are, could be written and used.

He lit the flame that led to the invention of the calculus, which is the mathematics of changing rates and speeds and quantities.

The door to modern science opened through the mind of Archimedes.

But probably the most important thing Archimedes gave to the world was a logical way of *thinking* about mathematics. Like his predecessor, Euclid, he had a way of taking things in order, step by step, so that he could prove or disprove his ideas as he went along.

Archimedes lived in one of the greatest civilizations the world has ever known, among many brilliant minds, and yet he was outstanding even there.

What was the world of Archimedes like?

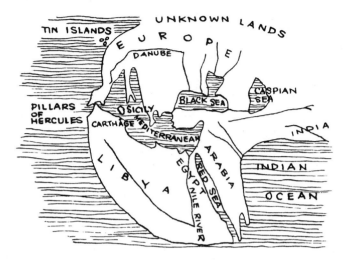

(2)

The World of Archimedes

IF YOU LOOK at a map of the world, you will find Sicily in the Mediterranean Sea — an island off the toe of Italy.

A map of the world in Archimedes' time looked like the one on this page.

To the north, in Europe, lived many half-civilized tribes who still wore skins for clothes, and lived in caves or crude houses.

9

To the west, where the Mediterranean Sea flowed through the Pillars of Hercules, there were only endless oceans, as far as anyone knew.

To the south, past the thin strip of civilized Egypt, there were great deserts, and beyond these, explorers who sailed down the coast told of thick and steaming jungles inhabited by savages they called "gorillas."

East of the Mediterranean Sea there were civilized countries and great cities, but beyond these stretched a wild and barren land through which an occasional caravan traveled to trade for silk in the Far East, which had a great civilization of its own.

If you look at the map of Archimedes' world beside the map of our world it seems very small, but to the people who lived then it seemed much larger than ours does to us.

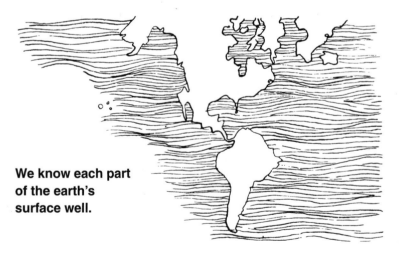

We know each part of the earth's surface well.

A jet plane can travel around our world in a day.

A satellite can make the journey in minutes.

But in the third century before Christ, traveling from one place to another took weeks or months or even years.

There were very few good roads. The Romans were the first to understand the value of roads paved so that they were not a sea of mud in the winter and a desert of dust and rocks in the summer.

There were no fast ships.

During their whole lives most people never traveled more than a few miles from the places where they were born.

There was no television or radio, telephone or telegraph. There were no newspapers or printing presses. But, somehow, ideas got around.

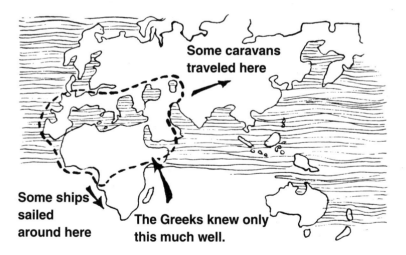

Some caravans traveled here

Some ships sailed around here

The Greeks knew only this much well.

The ideas of the Greeks influenced the thinking of the Western world forever after. They influenced our science, our laws, and our arts. They laid a foundation for our thinking about ethics — that is, the way we behave and the things we think are right.

The Greeks were different from all the people who came before them and from most of those who followed. Nobody knows for sure *why* they were so different, or what started them thinking in such a special way.

What would it have been like, to live in Greece then? What would it be like, to grow up with Archimedes?

If you were a boy in Archimedes' time, growing up on the island of Sicily or in almost any Greek city, your mind was alive with curiosity. You expected strange and wonderful things to happen and you watched for them in the streets and on the docks, in the market place and everywhere else.

Syracuse was a busy city. Sicily was an island colony of Greece, far from the Greek mainland and the islands clustered near it, but close to Italy and not too far from the coast of Africa. The docks of Syracuse were crowded with Greek ships from all over the Mediterranean — ships loaded with fish from the Black Sea and grain from Egypt, with many kinds of goods from the factories of Athens.

The markets were jammed with merchants selling goods; the narrow streets were crowded with busy, hurrying citizens; workmen filled the prosperous shipyards which rang with talk and laughter and the sound of saws and hammers.

The sea was the life of Syracuse. It was work, and the road to her door. If you were a boy in Syracuse you would spend many hours on the docks, watching the workmen and the sailors, watching the ships come and go. You would ask why a sail curved in the wind, and why a boat was built in a particular way. If you were Archimedes, you probably asked why it floated at all.

Nobody was too busy to stop and answer questions. Because the Greeks thought that wondering was the beginning of thinking, they asked questions about everything, whether useful or useless.

What was the world made of?

Why was it like it was?

What were the reasons for anything?

They asked and answered and argued. The Greeks argued about everything. They argued in the streets and in the market, at meetings and on the docks, in the theater, at home, and in the baths. But they didn't argue angrily with each other, and they listened as much as they talked — and that is the sensible way to argue. They were quick to respect a reasonable argument and to laugh at a silly one.

If you were a boy in Archimedes' time you were taught to think before you went to school.

You started learning to think when you were very small, at home. Even when you were small, you were expected to be reasonable.

Archimedes, like the other boys, was in the care of his mother or a nurse until he was almost eight. He lived, like all younger children in a Greek household, in the women's quarters. When only the family was at home, everyone used the courtyard and the main hall of the house, but a child never went there when his father had guests.

Archimedes and his friends played hide-and-seek and tug-of-war. They played jackstones with knucklebones, and rolled hoops and ran races. They had swings and toy carts, and maybe even a wagon big enough to hitch to a dog or a pet goat.

When Archimedes was good, his nurse told him stories from *Aesop's Fables*. When he was bad, she frightened him with ghost stories about a horrible bugaboo called Mormo, or about Empersa, a hobgoblin who could disguise himself as anything, or about Acco, who carried off bad children in a sack.

Because he lived so long ago, nobody knows much about Archimedes' family. It is known that his father, Phidias, was an astronomer who spent his life investigating the distances to the sun and moon. It is known that Archimedes was a relative of Hiero II, the King of Syracuse, and might even have spent part of his life living in the king's palace.

When he was eight, Archimedes started school. Now he was put in the special charge of one of the slaves of the household, who followed him everywhere — to school, in the streets, and even at home — carrying his books and other belongings. But the slave had a more important job than merely carrying books.

He saw that Archimedes did not get into mischief or fall in with bad companions. He taught him manners — the proper way to eat and walk, to sit and dress. He taught him to rise in the presence of his elders, to be polite in any circumstances, to be modest instead of boastful. And he taught him the greatest ideal of the Greeks: self-restraint, which means self-control, and discipline, which means order in thinking and acting.

By the time he started school, Archimedes was supposed to know *how* to think. Now he was given more things to think about.

Maybe you have an idea that more than two thousand years ago there were not so many things to learn. It is true that nowadays, even before you get to high school, you know things that would have astonished and bewildered the most brilliant minds of Archimedes' day. You know more because there is more to know, but you don't think any better. You have more to know because the people before you have wondered and thought and experimented and made mistakes and proved things.

NO. it's because it's already been thought for us.

But even two thousand years ago in Greece there was much to learn.

Before the Greeks, there was no *true* science. The Egyptians had a *practical* science, but that was different. For the Egyptians, science had to have an everyday purpose. Geometry was useful in surveying. Astronomy was useful in predicting the flood season of the Nile. But the Greeks loved knowledge for its own sake.

Many of the things they knew were of no practical use to them. Many of the things were forgotten, after them, for hundreds of years. And many of those things, rediscovered, were a new beginning to modern science and philosophy.

The Greeks knew geometry. They felt that a person could think more clearly and logically if he had learned it. The great Greek teacher, Plato, who lived more than a hundred years before Archimedes was born, wrote over the entrance to his school, "Let no man destitute of geometry enter my doors." Some of the Greek books on geometry are still used today.

The Greeks knew perfectly well that the world was round. They also knew that it was suspended in space, and they knew something about the movement of the planets. They had a map of the heavens and could even predict an eclipse.

Some Greeks taught that all living things, even man himself, had begun in the sea.

Some Greek scientists believed that everything was made of atoms, tiny particles moving through empty space.

They knew that the earth turns on its axis once in 24 hours to make a day. And they knew the circumference or distance around the earth.

They had books on astronomy, politics, law, physics, poetry, music, biology, and more. There was a lot to learn.

Girls never went to school, but studied with their mothers or nurses. Boys went to school every day.

Like almost everybody else in Greece, Archimedes got up at daybreak and put on his short woolen tunic and his sandals. Breakfast was a roll, dipped in wine and water. After Archimedes had eaten that, he

17

walked to school with his slave, through the narrow, crooked streets of Syracuse. Greeks never rode in the city unless they were ill or starting on a long journey. It was considered "showing off."

School was in the teacher's house. If the weather was good, the boys sat on benches in the courtyard. In poor weather they sat inside on the floor, leaning against the wall, their eyes watering a little in the smoke from the iron warming-brazier.

Archimedes scratched his letters on a wax-covered wooden tablet with a sharp-pointed iron graver. When he could write very well he was allowed to write on papyrus with a pen made from a reed, and ink made of gum and soot.

He learned to read the names and write the forms of the letters, which looked like this:

α'	β'	γ'	δ'	ϵ'	ς'	ς'	η'	θ'
1	2	3	4	5	6	7	8	9
ι'	κ'	λ'	μ'	ν'	ξ'	o'	π'	ς'
10	20	30	40	50	60	70	80	90
ρ'	σ'	τ'	υ'	ϕ'	χ'	ψ'	ω'	λ'
100	200	300	400	500	600	700	800	900

A little mark next to the letter, or over it, meant that it was being used as a numeral.

And he learned the values of the letters, for they were numerals, too.

At first, he did his figuring with the help of a counting board and pebbles, and then he learned to work directly with the clumsy Greek numbers.

He worked geometry problems in a layer of damp sand that was spread on the floor.

He studied Homer, who was a poet and wrote history,

and Aesop, who wrote fables,

and Solon, who wrote about the laws.

He studied astronomy and music and drawing.

He learned how to play the lyre and how to sing and dance.

He learned military tactics and how to use weapons.

This seems like a lot of education, but Archimedes and his schoolmates were going to be Greek citizens, and the Greeks expected a lot from their citizens. Every single one was called on to take an active part in the government of his own city-state. He voted, he took turns in helping to make the laws, he acted as a juror in the courts. If he appeared in a case of law, he had to plead his own cause, or defend himself. He was expected to help keep order and detect crime. He had to do a period of military service.

Because the Greeks believed that a good mind needed a good body, Archimedes, along with all the other boys, spent a great part of the day in a sunny, open field called the "palestra."

He learned wrestling and boxing, running and jumping, and casting the spear. He learned swimming and diving. The boys didn't wear clothes in the palestra, but only a thick coat of oil which they scraped off before they went swimming.

As the boys grew up, the ones who were going to be farmers and tradesmen, merchants, sailors, or craftsmen finished their schooling and dropped out to start work.

The boys who were left spent most of their time in the palestra or the gymnasium, talking, talking, talking. Now they no longer had a schoolmaster. The great thinkers of the day came to talk to them. They learned law and ethics. They discovered the richness of their language and the many ways of using it. And they read endlessly.

It is surprising how popular and how common books were among the Greeks, almost 1,800 years before the invention of the printing press. Every book was written by hand. Every sheet of paper was handmade. The sheets were pasted together at the edges to make rolls 150 feet long. Can you imagine reading a page 150 feet long? That's about ten times as long as an ordinary room.

When Archimedes was a student, the head of the great library at Alexandria had a wonderful idea. He decided to divide the long, clumsy rolls into short rolls called "books." Books were kept in cases like this.

See that open top? Very often, mice lived in with the books.

Archimedes must have wandered often through the market place, where whole sections were devoted to stalls selling books. The great poems of the day were published, and so were the plays and the ideas of scholars and teachers. Greek books were sent abroad, too, with other trade goods, all over the Mediterranean.

Often Archimedes went to the theater with his friends, and then to the baths in the late afternoon before he went home to supper and bed.

How did the Greeks happen to have time for so much exercising and going to the theater, so much shopping and walking about, so much talking and looking and asking?

Were they rich?

A laborer earned from six to ten cents a day, while a skilled craftsman earned about twenty cents. An educated man, like an architect, might earn thirty cents.

But, for one thing, their lives were not as complicated as ours are.

Their climate was easy and their wants were simple.

Most people wore merely a simple, woolen robe, or chiton. Unless a person was rich, this was also his blanket at night. In winter he wore a woolen cloak over his chiton, and he used that for an extra blanket.

The Greeks had very little furniture in their houses. They walked where they wanted to go. They ate very simply. They did not need, or even want to be bothered with, as many things as we do.

But still, there was another reason why Greek citizens had so much leisure. The word "citizens" is the clue.

Only some of the people of Greece were citizens. Most of the people who lived in that country were slaves. Some of the slaves were foreigners. Some were Greeks who had been captured in wars with other city-states. (The Greeks so dearly loved to argue that their cities were always fighting among themselves, and that, in the end, was their downfall.)

Most of the actual work in Greece was done by slaves. They worked in the mines and in the factories, on the docks and in the shops. They worked as servants and policemen, as soldiers and accountants and secretaries and teachers. Slaves made it possible for the Greek citizens to devote themselves to learning and to the arts.

As Archimedes grew older, he spent more and more time thinking and studying and learning and writing. He thought so little about himself that he had to be fed because he forgot to eat, and carried to the baths because he didn't want to stop to wash, and even dressed and undressed, because if he was in the middle of a problem he forgot his clothes.

But when he was young he lived like his friends and fellows, going to the gymnasium and the baths, arguing in the market and at the theater, reading, looking, asking, and thinking.

(3)

Alexandria!

WHEN Archimedes had learned as much as he could in Syracuse, he left Sicily for the only time in his life and went to Egypt to study in Alexandria.

Alexandria was the greatest city in the ancient world. It was still young when Archimedes went there; it had been founded in 332 B.C. by Alexander the Great. When Alexander died, his generals divided among themselves the empire he had won.

Ptolemy took Egypt and made Alexandria the fountainhead of Greek art and learning.

He built the largest library in the world up to that time, with more than half a million books, and he founded the Museum, which opened in about 300 B.C. Ptolemy invited the most learned men in the ancient world to come there to live and work and teach. Nowadays we would call Ptolemy's Museum at Alexandria a great university. It was the center of Greek learning for a thousand years.

The Museum was the first scientific institution in world history to be founded and supported by a government. Ptolemy brought together here the greatest group of scientists of the times, and paid their salaries. This was something new. Here the scientists had no financial problems, no worries about supporting themselves.

They were free to devote themselves to ideas, and all around them were brilliant minds with whom to discuss and argue these ideas. The laboratories and the library were crammed with everything they needed for study and research.

This was the beginning of the kind of scientific research we know today, and the work that was done at the Museum was the core of all scientific knowledge for the next two thousand years, until modern scientists picked up the job.

From all over Greece, from all over the Mediterranean, the young men who wanted to study science, who wanted to be engineers, architects, astronomers, doctors, or mathematicians came to study with the greatest group of scientific specialists in the world. It was an age of technical training as important to its day as the one we live in now is to us.

Archimedes could hardly wait for the season of storms to be over, so that he could find a ship bound for Alexandria. The Greeks never sailed in the winter when the winds were wild and the sea uncertain. The sailing season began in the spring when the stars called the Pleiades appeared.

Every day Archimedes hurried to the docks and talked to the captains, until he found one bound for Alexandria, who would take him as a passenger. Archimedes packed the few things he needed, took formal leave of his friends and relatives, and offered sacrifices to the goddess Artemis and the twins, Castor and Polydeuces, the gods who protected travelers on the sea.

The Greeks were good sailors, but a sea journey was a dangerous thing. They had no compass or any charts to guide them, and the Mediterranean was full of pirates. Greek freighters were small, wooden ships called "round ships." Because round ships had only a square sail that could not be shifted, the ship always had to sail with the wind. It did not even have a keel to keep it steady in the sea.

26

The Greek Empire was scattered all over the Mediterranean, and the sea was the only road from one colony to another. Most Greeks were at home on the water, even though they never felt really safe. They avoided the open sea if they could, staying close to the coast or sailing from island to island, trying always to be at anchor when darkness came.

It probably took Archimedes sixteen or seventeen days to sail from Syracuse to Alexandria. Maybe he walked about the deck of the little ship and watched the wind in the sail, and the changing colors of the sea. Sometimes, with the sailors, he held his breath as another ship came into sight along the horizon, sighed with relief that it was not a pirate ship, and after it had passed, watched it fall away. What sailor could not know that the earth was round!

Maybe even then he had to be reminded to eat a little salt fish and some bread dipped in wine or olive oil. Usually he ate with the sailors, enjoying the meat cooked on deck in a big and bubbling pot, with the ship's boy doing the cooking.

Sometimes the boatswain played tunes on his whistle. Sometimes the sailors played pitch-and-toss on deck, or manned the clumsy oars when the wind died or went against them.

Not for Archimedes the shelter under the poop-deck awning at night! Wrapped in his woolen cloak, he lay on his mattress under the stars, wondering how far away they were, wondering if there was a pattern in their swing across the heavens.

How impatient he was to get to Alexandria!

Did he see, first, from far out at sea, the famous Pharos lighthouse, standing thirty or forty stories high

or even higher at the entrance to the harbor? Nobody knows for sure whether it had been built by the time Archimedes came to Alexandria, but it might have been: an early lighthouse and one of the Seven Wonders of the Ancient World.

He gasped as they sailed into the great harbor. Certainly the harbor at Syracuse was nothing like this! At one side of the harbor entrance was Pharos Island, and standing proudly on a point of land at the other side was the royal palace of Ptolemy. Against the green of the palace gardens the royal war fleet rode at anchor. Near the other end of the park that stretched around the curve of the harbor, the captain pointed out the gleaming marble walls of the Museum itself.

Soon they were coming into the docks of Alexandria, stretching in all directions, crowded with ships. There were ships from Spain and Africa, ships from the British Isles loaded with bars of tin, junks from China carrying silk, ships from the Indian Ocean loaded with spices and cotton. Archimedes had never seen such sights or smelled such smells. Alexandria!

He walked through the hot, crowded streets, trying to see and hear everything. There were people of every color, dressed in every color, speaking every language. But all around him he heard Greek, too. It was the daily language of all the great cities of the Mediterranean at that time, and Greeks seldom bothered learning other languages.

Slowly he made his way up from the docks and through the noisy streets until at last he came to the royal park, green and quiet, with beautiful tropical trees and gardens stretching out on every side. There were fountains playing, and lakes sparkling in the sun, and statues gleaming in the shrubbery. And there in the center was the Museum. Ptolemy wanted his thinkers to see beauty everywhere.

What did Archimedes study at Alexandria?

Certainly he went to the school of mathematics which Euclid had founded.

Euclid was a Greek, too. He was born about 330 B.C. and he died about 275 B.C., before Archimedes was old enough to come to Alexandria. Euclid's followers at the Museum carried on his work. His way of teaching and the textbooks that he wrote have been used for two thousand years. Archimedes and his fellow students must have studied them.

Euclid was a good mathematician, but what is even more important, he had a scholarly, brilliantly orderly mind. He had collected, slowly, carefully, and painstakingly, all the bits and pieces of geometrical learning that were known in the world of his day. He had arranged and rearranged them, in the way you would start putting together a giant jigsaw puzzle, until they began to form a picture.

Where there were pieces missing, he worked until he found — or made — pieces to fit. When Euclid finished, he had thirteen books, each written on a roll of parchment. He called his books *The Elements.*

Elements are the basic things from which everything else is made. Euclid's *Elements* were the basis of all the geometrical knowledge in the world for twenty centuries, until other mathematicians worked out different systems of geometry.

We still use Euclid's geometry for our calculations of actual things. But we need other kinds of geometry for our calculations of things Euclid probably never dreamed of measuring, such as relationships between time and space and energy.

In its first years the Museum produced the three greatest mathematicians of the ancient world: Euclid, who founded the science of geometry, and Archimedes and Apollonius, who studied together at the school. These three shaped the plan along which all mathematics developed for twenty centuries. Before, it had been a branch of philosophy. In addition, they made it into an important science of its own.

Archimedes' teacher of mathematics at the Museum was Conon of Samos. Conon was not only a mathematician, but one of the great early astronomers. He was a student of the sun's eclipses, and he discovered the constellation Coma Berenices.

Archimedes attended lectures in astronomy and physics, as well as mathematics. In addition, if he wanted them, there were classes in geography, zoology, anatomy, medicine, rhetoric, and literature.

Whatever they were studying, the students first became familiar with all the known facts about the subject. Then they all worked together to try and learn new things.

Archimedes was so busy at the Museum that often he did not leave it for days, but hurried back and forth from his living quarters to the lecture halls, hardly hearing the voices around him, or the cries of the animals in the anatomy laboratories.

Sometimes he worked in the quiet rooms of the great library, helping to copy by hand the famous books that were there. Some had grown old and tattered.

Some had been badly copied and were hard to read. The copies which the librarians and students made in the library at Alexandria were the standard editions which all the libraries in the ancient world used and from which they made their own copies.

Sometimes with his teacher, Conon, and his friend, Eratosthenes, he climbed the tower to the astronomical observatory. The three watched the stars together and helped take observations of the sun.

Eratosthenes, like Conon, settled in Alexandria and spent his life at the Museum. He became head of the library. He measured the circumference and tilt of the earth, and the sizes and distances of the sun and moon. He also became a great geographer, and was the first to indicate latitude and longitude on a map.

For the rest of his life, Archimedes exchanged ideas with the friends he had made at the Museum. Most of them became great mathematicians, and they jokingly rated each other as first-, second-, or third-class in their profession.

The first-class group were called "alphas." (Remember Archimedes' boyhood lessons? Alpha was the Greek "1," as well as the letter "A.") Archimedes was an "alpha."

The great Eratosthenes was only a "beta," or second-class mathematician. You can see that these young Greek scientists were pretty strict graders!

(Where do you think our way of marking A, B, C, and so on came from?)

Sometimes the friends wandered together about the city. They enjoyed the great bazaar, with its stalls of goods and treasures from all over the world. They went to concerts and the theater, the gymnasium and the baths.

Sometimes they traveled by barge down the Nile River, through the most fertile farmland in the world. They visited Egyptian cities that were then thousands of years old.

Every year the Nile overflowed and, as soon as the waters receded, the farmers plowed their fields and planted their crops. The sun was so warm and the Nile Valley was so fertile that they raised two or three crops a year.

But water was a problem. For many months there was no rain and the farmers had to carry the water by hand, bucket by bucket, up out of the river into their fields.

Archimedes watched them again and again, and

34

thought that there must be a better way to do it. He planned and he made diagrams. He went to a carpenter and explained what he wanted. The carpenter shook his head, because he had never seen anything like it. But he followed Archimedes' plan.

What he built is called the Archimedean screw.

It worked like this.

A wooden screw, like a long corkscrew, was fitted into a cylinder-shaped case. The bottom of the screw was placed in the water, and the top rested over land. At the top of the screw there was a handle.

When Archimedes turned the handle, the screw turned, too. As long as the screw was placed in the

water at the right angle, when the screw turned it raised the water from one spiral up to the next. Up came the water out of the Nile, until it flowed out over the land into the fields.

The farmers of Egypt are still using the Archimedean screw to irrigate their fields, after more than two thousand years. Other people around the world use it, too. In Holland it is used in reverse, to drain the land and put water back into the sea.

Some people say that Archimedes did not invent his screw for raising water from the Nile, but for pumping out the bilges of King Hiero's great ships, and that the Nile farmers heard about it later.

Archimedes' screw is also used today in spiral conveyors designed to lift grain or sand, and in some high-speed tools.

It may seem odd that a turning screw can lift and move water (or anything else), but it can.

A screw is a machine. A machine is any mechanical device that helps us do work. (We'll talk more about what this means in the next chapter.)

A screw has two main parts.

This is the *body*.

This is the *thread*.

axis ----

The thread is wrapped around the body

Anything touching the threads moves along them, up the axis of the screw.

The center line of the body is called the *axis*.

As the screw turns, anything in contact with the thread moves along the axis, from crest to crest of the threads. (Don't the threads look something like waves? The peak of each is the crest.)

All screws have the same kind of work to do.

When you put a screw into a board, the wood moves up the axis of the screw, from crest to crest of the thread.

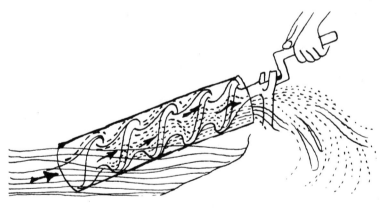

When Archimedes turned the handle of his screw, the water moved up the axis, from crest to crest of the thread, until it flowed out the top.

37

Archimedes' screw was the ancestor of another kind of water screw, the propeller. By pushing water back, a propeller moves a boat forward, like this.

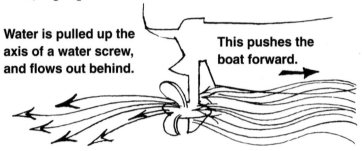

Water is pulled up the axis of a water screw, and flows out behind.

This pushes the boat forward.

Propellers on airplanes are called air screws. They move a plane forward by pushing air back, like this.

Air flows up the axis of an air screw, and out behind it. This pushes the plane forward.

Did you think a machine depended on a motor? Long before there were motors or engines, Archimedes was building wonderful machines.

(4)

Archimedes and His Lever

WHEN Archimedes returned to Syracuse, his mind
was full of the things he had learned in Alexandria.
The days did not seem long enough for exploring all
the ideas he had, and working out all the proofs.

He sat for hours, drawing his diagrams in the
sand on the floor of his workroom. Most geometers
worked this way in ancient times. They had no pen-
cils or erasers. Papyrus was too scarce to scribble on

and throw away, and it was difficult to change or correct a diagram cut into a clay tablet.

But if you have ever drawn in the damp sand on the beach, you can see why using the floor was a good, practical idea. Archimedes drew swiftly, and erased by smoothing the sand.

When he was not in his workroom, but sitting by the fire in the evening, he drew diagrams in the ashes on the hearth.

Even in the bath, he traced geometrical figures on his oil-covered skin.

Sometimes he amused himself by working out geometrical problems and proofs with actual things. That's what experimenting is — proving ideas with things, instead of with words or diagrams.

He and King Hiero enjoyed many arguments over this. Archimedes said that pure reasoning was the most beautiful thing in the world, that nothing was more perfect than an idea, reasoned through from beginning to end. King Hiero said that mathematical ideas were nothing in themselves until they were applied to practical things that everyone could understand and appreciate.

Archimedes pretended to scorn the idea of reducing the pure science of mathematics to the more practical science of mechanics, but he must have enjoyed it because he contrived some wonderful things.

One kind of mechanics deals with all kinds of

machines and how they work. But scientists think of mechanics in another way, too.

Mechanics is the action of forces on things —
on solid things like metal,
on liquid things like water,
or on gases, like air.

Force is power or energy.

Whenever a force makes something move, scientists say that work is done.

When water turns a water wheel, work is done.

When a jet engine pushes a rocket, work is done.

When you pick up a piece of candy, work is done. That may seem queer, but any movement is work, in the scientific meaning of the word.

One day, when Archimedes and Hiero were having their favorite argument, Archimedes said that it was quite easy to apply mathematics to real things.

"In fact," he said firmly, "I have figured it out carefully, and there is no weight, anywhere, that could not be moved if enough force were applied."

He waved his arm grandly under King Hiero's nose. "Had I but another earth on which to stand, my friend," he said, "I could move this earth itself."

Hiero shouted with laughter. "You are perfectly safe in making such a statement because you have no possible way to prove it!"

"It would be as simple as this." Archimedes snapped his fingers. "Not having a place to stand, I cannot move the earth, but give me some other great weight and I will move it myself with no help from any man."

Hiero thought for a minute. Then he laughed again.

"I have in my fleet," he said, "a new ship with three masts, so big and heavy that so far the combined strength of all my slaves who work on the docks has not been enough to move it from the slip. Move *that* weight singlehanded, Archimedes, and I will believe your story."

Archimedes bowed. "I accept your challenge," he said, and went away to work on the problem.

News of the challenge spread about the city until everyone was talking about it. When Archimedes announced that he was ready, King Hiero named a day for the test. From early that morning the docks were jammed with people, and so were the nearby

rooftops. It looked as if everyone in Syracuse had come to watch the show.

There in the slip sat the great ship. It was heavy enough in itself, but King Hiero had added an additional load. It carried full freight, and many passengers besides.

Archimedes did not seem in the least troubled. He was busy with a series of ropes and wheels that ran from the ship to a helix that was fixed on the dock. The helix looked like a big screw with a handle on it.

After Archimedes had checked the ropes and wheels, he stood calmly, his fingers on the handle.

"Let me know when you are ready," called Hiero anxiously. "Do you need more time? Would you like someone to help you? Or is this a joke?"

"I am ready now," said Archimedes, smiling. He started turning the handle.

The crowd laughed and shouted. Then, with a great gasp, they leaned forward to look more closely. The ship was moving!

Archimedes was using only one hand, slowly turning the handle, drawing the cords around the helix. But still, the ship was moving! She came out of the slip slowly, but as smoothly as if she had been at sea, sailing under a steady wind.

A roar went up from the crowd. "Who said he was a little crazy?" they asked each other indignantly. (Almost all of them had.) Now they looked at him in awe.

Archimedes motioned for the king to take the handle. Hiero turned it nervously, but still the ship moved smoothly and steadily. He stopped, and held up his hand.

"Everyone hear this," he shouted. "I order, from this day on, that Archimedes is to be believed in anything he says."

What does the pulley that moved the ship have to do with Archimedes' idea of a lever that could move the world?

A pulley is a lever. The laws of pulleys and levers that Archimedes discovered gave people everywhere the strength to work at many things.

But what is a lever, anyway?

A screw driver is a lever. So is a crowbar or a hammer. So is an oar.

44

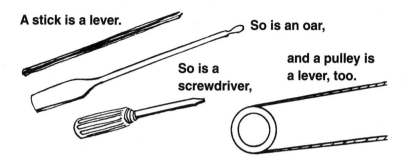

A stick is a lever.

So is an oar,

So is a screwdriver,

and a pulley is a lever, too.

A lever is a machine. Do you think that a machine has to have some kind of power? You are right, but the power does not have to come from an engine or a motor. *You* can be the power.

A machine is any mechanical device man uses to help him do work. But a machine can only do work after work has been applied to the machine. You have to add something to a machine to get work out of it. You have to add force.

A stick can be a machine, but not by itself.

A rope can be a machine, but not by itself.

You have to add force. Force is a push or a pull.

45

Archimedes added force to his machine when he turned the handle.

What good is a machine if you have to do work to make the machine work?

When he moved the ship with one hand, Archimedes showed what a machine could do.

A machine is any device that helps us to do work more easily.

If you had to drag a bag of sand up a steep and bumpy cliff, it would be very hard work.

If there were a flight of stairs going up the cliff, you wouldn't have to work quite as hard to get the sand to the top. (Did you know that a flight of stairs was a machine?)

If there was an elevator up the cliff, your work would be easier still. You would hardly have to work at all to get the sand up.

The help that a machine gives us is called "mechanical advantage."

46

Sometimes we gain mechanical advantage by using a small force and making it move through a great distance. Archimedes used a small force (his own strength),

moved through a great distance (many, many yards of rope),

when he turned the handle

that wound in the ropes

that pulled the ship.

Some machines do their work by using a large force, moved through a small distance.

The explosion of a large force (gasoline) to move the pistons of an engine up and down, is an example of this.

All real machines help to make something move.

Some move large things with a small force.

Some make things move faster.

Some change the direction in which something is moving.

Machines are sometimes called by different names, depending on the jobs they do.

Those with no moving parts, like a saw or a screw driver, are called *tools*.

A machine that changes one kind of energy — like gasoline — into mechanical power that moves things is usually called an *engine* or *motor*.

A machine that changes mechanical power — like water flowing over a dam — into electrical power is

47

called a *generator*.

But whether it's a tool, an engine, or a generator, a true machine always produces some kind of motion.

Do you think of television sets or radios as machines?

Do they produce motion?

No. Their job is to give information. Because they tell you something instead of doing something, they are not really machines.

When Archimedes set himself the problem, *to move a given weight by a given force,* he discovered some interesting things about the machine that he was using, the lever.

He discovered that a lever had to be free to move on some point.

Here is a lever.

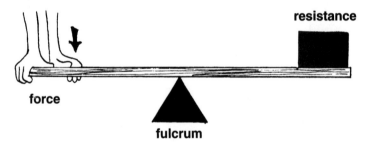

The work done on it — the push or pull — is the *force*.

The work to be done is the *resistance*.

The point on which the lever turns or moves is the *fulcrum*.

48

But the force, the resistance, and the fulcrum do not always have to be in the same place in relation to each other. If you change their positions, they do different jobs.

Look at this.

If you use a stick to pry up a rock, like this,

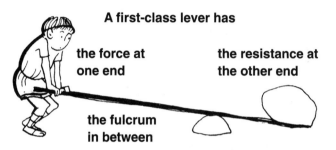

A first-class lever has

the force at one end

the resistance at the other end

the fulcrum in between

the force (you) and the resistance (the rock) are moving in opposite directions, with the fulcrum between them. This is called a *first-class lever*.

A first-class lever can gain force, or change speed or direction. A stick or a crowbar is a first-class lever. So is a pair of scissors.

If you have a *second-class lever*,
the fulcrum is at one end,
the resistance is in the middle,
and the force is at the other end.

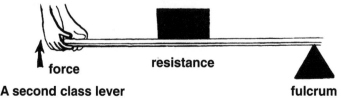

force

resistance

fulcrum

A second class lever

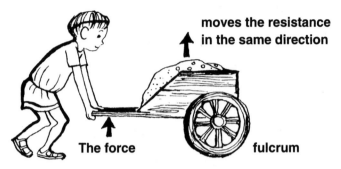

moves the resistance
in the same direction

The force   fulcrum

A wheelbarrow is a second-class lever. Can you see that when force is applied, it moves the resistance in the same direction? A second-class lever gains force. How else could you carry a load of gravel in a wheel barrow? An oar is a second-class lever, too. How else could you pull a boat through the water?

A *third-class* lever has
the fulcrum at one end,
the force in the middle,
and the resistance at the other end.

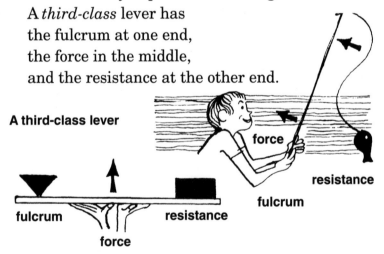

A third-class lever

force

resistance

fulcrum   resistance   fulcrum

force

The force and the resistance move in the same direction. A shovel is a third-class lever. So is a baseball bat. So is a fishing rod.

50

A pulley is a kind of lever, too. A pulley makes it possible for the force to act continuously, and so is very handy because the work doesn't have to stop until new force is applied.

Maybe Archimedes used this kind of pulley to move King Hiero's ship.

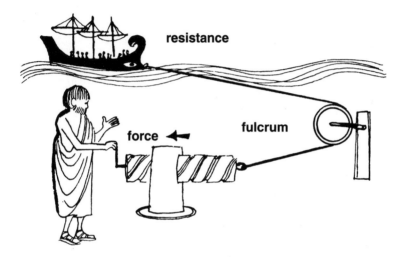

Can you figure out which class it belongs to? (Of course, Archimedes could never have done the job with only one pulley. He had to use a series of pulleys.)

The force is supplied at one side. (Archimedes is the force.)

The resistance is at the other. (The ship is the resistance.)

The fulcrum is the pulley wheel.

51

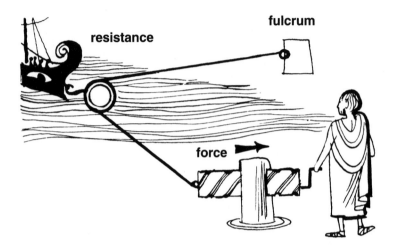

Maybe Archimedes used this kind of pulley.

Can you see why it is a second-class lever?

A wheel and axle are a kind of lever, too. Can you see why?

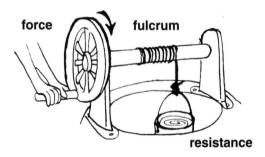

Actually, only two kinds of machines, in many, many combinations, make up all the mechanical devices in the world.

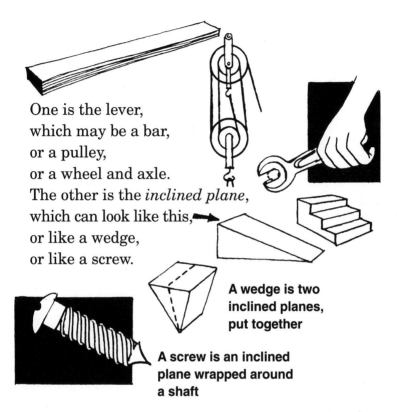

One is the lever,
which may be a bar,
or a pulley,
or a wheel and axle.
The other is the *inclined plane*,
which can look like this,
or like a wedge,
or like a screw.

**A wedge is two
inclined planes,
put together**

**A screw is an inclined
plane wrapped around
a shaft**

When Archimedes built his screw for raising water out of the Nile, and his pulleys for moving King Hiero's ship, he used both machines to help him do the work.

Do you think that Archimedes *could* have moved the earth if he had had a place to stand?

Probably he could. But scientists have figured out that his lever would have to be 88,000,000,000,000,-000,000,000 miles long!

(5)

Archimedes and King Hiero's Crown

KING HIERO was very pleased. He had ordered a new crown of pure gold, and the goldsmith, bowing low, had just delivered it himself. The workmanship was beautiful, and the crown sat comfortably on the king's head.

Maybe it was just a little *too* comfortable and that was what started King Hiero's suspicions.

"Shouldn't a solid gold crown as large as this one be just a little heavier?" he asked himself.

King Hiero had given the goldsmith a lump of pure gold with which to make the crown. He knew just what the gold weighed.

"Perhaps," he said anxiously to himself, "I ought to weigh the crown to see if he has used all the gold."

It wasn't that the king didn't have plenty of gold; he just couldn't bear the idea of being cheated.

The crown weighed exactly what the lump of gold had weighed, so the goldsmith *must* have used it all.

Or had he?

The king paced his courtyard, staring absentmindedly at the statues and through the fountains.

Suppose that the goldsmith had used only part of the gold, and mixed it with enough silver to weigh the same as the gold the king had given him? Nobody would be able to see the difference, and the goldsmith would have the rest of the gold for himself.

Hiero sent for the goldsmith, who protested that he would never, never cheat the king. The idea was unthinkable! Still, Hiero was uneasy about the new crown. He didn't even enjoy wearing it.

Then one day he sent for Archimedes. Archimedes was annoyed. He was in the middle of an interesting problem, and he sent back word that he couldn't interrupt his thinking for foolishness. But the king was determined. His messenger insisted that Archimedes come to the palace. Reluctantly Archimedes went.

"You always seem able to answer any problem, Archimedes," Hiero said, "so I shall give you this one. Find out for me whether my crown is solid gold, or if that scoundrel of a goldsmith has mixed the gold with silver."

Archimedes took the gold crown home with him.

He looked at it and he weighed it and he measured it. From the king's treasury he borrowed another piece of gold exactly like the one the goldsmith had been given. He weighed and measured that.

He sat looking at the crown and the gold for hours.

He put them away and tried to get back to his other problem, but somehow he couldn't concentrate on it. He kept thinking of the crown. There *must* be a way to find out if it was pure gold!

He spent days, just sitting, staring at it.

He forgot to eat unless his slaves fed him.

He sat, staring into the dark at night, until the slaves came in and lit the braziers.

He didn't bother to wash or change his clothes. He began to look so dirty and draggled and unkempt that finally two of his slaves picked him up and carried him off to the baths. Another slave ran alongside with Archimedes' towel, a bottle of oil, and a fresh chiton.

"Put me down!" Archimedes shouted as they hurried him, struggling, through the crooked streets. "Put me down, I say! I have more important things to do!"

Heads popped out of second-story windows and over the edges of balconies. People were pushed and jostled against the buildings. Everyone asked everyone else what Archimedes was working on *this* time. All of Syracuse knew that when he was working on a problem he detested stopping for anything, even everyday things like eating or bathing.

His slaves carried Archimedes into the baths, stripped off his clothes, and started rubbing him vigorously with oil. The bath attendant filled the large, sunken tub full of warm water. He was so entertained by the shouts, roars, and sputterings of the famous scientist that he let too much water into the tub; it was full almost to overflowing.

As Archimedes resignedly stepped down into the tub and lowered himself into the water, some of it sloshed out onto the floor.

"Well," he thought. "How interesting! The tub was filled to the brim. So, when I stepped in, the amount of water I displaced spilled over the edge. I wonder if the water I displaced. . . ." A light leaped into his eyes. He gave a shout and splashed up out of the tub.

"Master," asked one of the slaves anxiously, "are you all right? *Master!* Where are you going? Come back, come back!"

For Archimedes, forgetting his clothes, forgetting everything but his new idea, had dashed out of the baths and was running naked down the street, back to his house, back to the crown.

"Eureka!" he was shouting. In Greek, this means, "I have found it!"

He plunged into the house and got out the crown and the lump of gold. He hardly noticed when his servants came panting in and wrapped a robe around him.

With fingers trembling in excitement, he filled a clay jar to the brim with water, and set it in a bowl to catch the overflow. Then he put the crown into the jar and carefully measured the amount of water that spilled over into the bowl.

Taking out the crown, he filled the jar to the brim again, and this time he put the lump of gold in. Again water spilled over into the bowl, and again he measured the amount.

Aha! Less water had spilled out this time! What did that mean? It meant that the crown took up more room than the lump of gold, so it had displaced more water.

Since the crown and the gold both weighed the same, if they were both solid gold they should displace the same amount of water. But suppose that the gold-smith had added silver to only part of the gold?

Silver is lighter than gold, so more silver would be needed to make an equal weight. Then, wouldn't the greater amount of silver that the smith used have to take up more space? If the crown were gold and silver mixed, it would be bigger than the lump of pure gold, so it would displace more water.

King Hiero was right. The goldsmith had cheated him!

What Archimedes discovered was really much more important than whether the goldsmith had cheated the king. A whole new field of experiments opened to his mind, and he discovered many interesting things.

First, he found a way to tell different substances apart.

Some materials are heavier than others. We say they are more *dense*.

Gold is heavier than iron.

Iron is heavier than wood.

Water is heavier than air.

What makes one thing weigh more than some-thing else? It is because gravity pulls harder on denser things than it does on less dense things.

Gravity pulls harder on a rock than on a feather the same size.

Gravity pulls harder on gold than on water, and harder on water than on wood.

Archimedes compared other things with the weight, or density, of an equal amount of water.

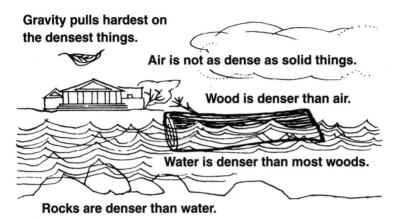

Gravity pulls hardest on the densest things.

Air is not as dense as solid things.

Wood is denser than air.

Water is denser than most woods.

Rocks are denser than water.

The weight of any substance, compared to the weight of the same amount, or *volume*, of water, is called its *specific gravity*.

Gold is 19 times heavier than the same volume of water. Its specific gravity is 19.3.

Air is about 7 times lighter than water. Its specific gravity is $\frac{1}{7}$.

During his experiments, Archimedes discovered that liquids have different densities, just as solid things do. (Gases have different densities, too.)

Water is more dense than oil. If you mix them, won't the oil always rise to the top of the water? That's because gravity is pulling on it less.

Very salty water is more dense than fresh water. If you drop an object into different liquids, it will sink more or less, depending on the density of the liquid. The denser the liquid is, the less the object will sink.

Try this.

Take a pencil stub, between 2 and 3 inches long. You can break one off, but be sure you have the end with the metal band. (It doesn't matter if the eraser is still there or not.)

Drop the pencil, metal end down, into a tall glass of water. The metal end will weight it so that it floats upright. Look carefully to see how much of the stub sticks out of the water.

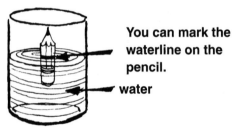

You can mark the waterline on the pencil.

water

Now fill another glass with kerosene or alcohol, and put the pencil in that, in the same positions. (Be sure to keep away from flames.)

How does the pencil float now? Doesn't it sink deeper? What does this tell you about the density of the two liquids?

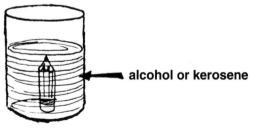

alcohol or kerosene

Water is denser, so it holds up any floating object (scientists would say "floating body") better than a less dense liquid does.

Some people notice that it is easier to swim in the ocean than in a lake. That is because salt water is denser, and holds them up better.

Archimedes made an instrument which told him, at a glance, the density of different liquids. The instrument is called a *hydrometer*, which means "water measurer."

Your floating pencil is actually a hydrometer. A simple hydrometer doesn't look so very different. It is a hollow glass or metal instrument, weighted at one end so that it floats upright.

On the shaft of the hydrometer is a scale, showing how far the hydrometer has sunk in the water.

If you know that the hydrometer sinks so far in one liquid, so far in another, so far in another,

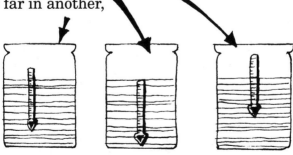

Which liquid is the densest?

you can tell the density of the liquid by looking at the scale.

If you have two liquids mixed, like water and acid in a storage battery, a hydrometer, by the depth it sinks, will tell you if there is the right amount of each. Acid is heavier than water; if the hydrometer floats too high, the battery needs water.

Today we use many different kinds of hydrometers for testing and measuring many substances.

While he was experimenting, Archimedes discovered something else very interesting. He noticed that things seem to lose weight under water. You have probably noticed this yourself.

Water has an upward-lifting force called *buoyancy*.

Air has buoyancy, too.

But why does buoyancy seem to work on some things and not on others? Why do some things float and others sink?

Why do some floating things stick way out of the water, and some things stick out just a little bit?

Try this experiment. Archimedes probably performed one almost exactly like it.

You need a large can,
and a smaller one. (Archimedes probably used
clay jars.)
You need a scale that shows ounces,
and a wooden block.
Weigh the block, and weigh the large can, empty.
Set the small can in the larger one and then fill
the small can carefully, to the very top, with water.

1. **Put the small can in the larger one.**
2. **Fill the small can to the very brim.**
3. **Put the block in the small can.**

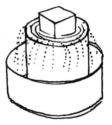

Now put the block in the small can, so that the
water it displaces flows over into the large can.

. Lift out the small can, with the block, and then
weigh the big can again, this time with the water in it.

How much does the water weigh?

What do you notice about the weight of the water
and the weight of the block?

You will see, just as Archimedes did, that a floating body displaces its own weight in water. The
weight it seems to lose equals the weight of the fluid
it displaces. It will sink until it displaces its own
weight in water.

65

Look at your floating block of wood.

If half of the block is under water, and half of it is sticking out, you know that the amount of water the block displaced —

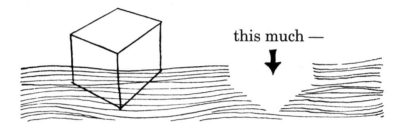

this much —

weighs as much as the whole block.

A cork is lighter than a block, so it displaces less water. Maybe only one-fourth of a floating cork is under the water.

Why do some things sink?

If you put a steel ball bearing in water, it will sink right away. It is heavier than the small volume of water it replaces.

But if you took the same amount of steel and shaped it into a boat, it would float. Can you see why?

Because now the steel takes up more room in the water. The bigger it is, the more water it displaces. You can keep loading things into a boat and it will still float, until it reaches the point where it weighs more than the water it displaces.

66

Did you ever see lines like this marked on the side of a freighter?

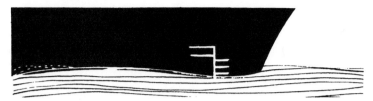

They show how deep in the water it is safe for the freighter to be when it is fully loaded. The amount of cargo a ship can carry is measured in *displacement* tons.

Water is heavy. Every cubic foot of water — this much —

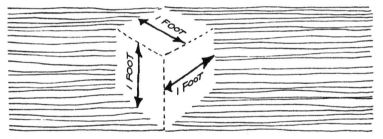

weighs 62.4 pounds. So every cubic foot of water can support that much weight and keep it floating.

Air has buoyancy, too.

A balloon rises because the gas it contains is lighter, or less dense, than the volume of air it displaces.

It will keep on rising until the weight of the air it displaces equals the weight of the balloon and its gas. (The higher you go, the less dense air becomes.)

67

Any objects will float if the buoyancy of the water or air that supports them is greater than the pull of gravity on them. They will sink if the buoyancy is less than the pull of gravity.

Archimedes' discoveries about buoyancy are summed up in "Archimedes' Principle": A body that is submerged partly or wholly in a fluid is buoyed up by a force equal to the weight of the fluid it displaces.

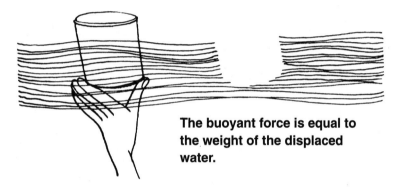

The buoyant force is equal to the weight of the displaced water.

Archimedes discovered other things about liquids, too.

Does the surface of the water in your drinking glass or your bathtub, or the soup in your soup bowl, look flat to you?

It isn't.

Archimedes proved that the surface of any fluid, when it is at rest, is curved like the surface of the earth, and that the center of that curve is the center of the earth.

Any sailor knows that the water in the sea follows the curve of the earth.

It looks like this,

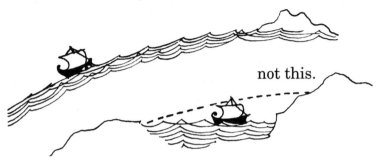

not this.

A sailor can see ships coming up into sight along the horizon.

He can see land, seeming to rise out of the sea as he gets closer.

The sea curves around the earth, and so does the water in your glass. Of course, the surface of the liquid in your glass or your soup bowl or even your bathtub is so small, compared to the great curve of the earth, that you can't see it just by looking.

Archimedes' experiments with liquids were the beginning of *hydrostatics*, the science which deals with the laws of nature that govern liquids at rest, and why they behave as they do, and the laws that govern the pressure of liquids and gases.

It was not until eighteen hundred years later that the French scientist, Blaise Pascal, added to the laws of hydrostatics.

(6)

Archimedes and Astronomy

THERE HAD BEEN many astronomers before the Greeks — but the astronomy of the Egyptians and the Babylonians was a practical astronomy. They made careful observations and kept careful records, not out of curiosity, but because these were helpful to them in everyday living. Their observations helped them predict eclipses, tides, and floods. They fixed boundaries by the shadows made by the sun. Knowing the positions of the stars and the sun helped them navigate their ships.

The Egyptians believed that the earth was a flat rectangle with Egypt in the middle, though they paid sharp attention to the positions of the stars. The great pyramids are placed so precisely, in relation to the important star positions at the time they were built, that their placing could not be accidental. Some of the pyramids seem to have been used as observatories as well as monuments.

The astronomers of India believed that the earth was inside a hollow iron sphere.

The Babylonians thought that the earth was a floating disk, and so did the early Greeks. But as they studied, their ideas began to change.

The Greeks approached astronomy as they did everything else — with wonder and curiosity. Astronomy had a special meaning to them. In the order and motion of the stars they saw the beauty and discipline that they valued above everything else. They tried to organize systematically the facts they could observe, and they were the first to develop theories about how the cosmos was arranged and how it worked.

Do you know that word *cosmos?* We use it today when we are talking about the universe, but it began as a Greek word, *kosmos,* which meant an "orderly and harmonious arrangement." The Greeks could see from the beginning that there was not only a grandeur about the stars, but an order and discipline. They tried, by careful observation and the

71

crude means of measuring that they had, to *suppose* (scientists say, "to construct hypotheses") what was happening in the heavens. Then they tried to prove their hypotheses with geometry.

The Greeks felt sure that the moon's light was really reflected sunlight. So they figured out that the shadow which crossed the moon's surface during an

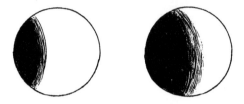

eclipse was the shadow of the earth, coming between the sun and the moon.

Aristotle, the tutor of Alexander the Great, pointed out that since the shadow of the earth on the moon was curved, the earth itself must be curved and have the form of a sphere.

From the time he was a boy, Archimedes was fascinated with astronomy. He loved to sit and watch Phidias working with his simple instruments, trying to calculate first the size, then the distance, of the sun and the moon.

Archimedes' two closest friends in Alexandria — Conon, his teacher, and Eratosthenes, his fellow student — both became famous astronomers. Archimedes spent many hours working with them.

In the third century before Christ, astronomers had none of the tools that astronomers today have. They had no telescopes, because they had no lenses. They had no radio signals, no spectroscopes, no inferometers, no cameras or computers. They didn't even have a real clock.

They had only their sharp powers of observation, their curiosity and great patience. They waited for months, comparing the phases of the moon, and for years, observing the shadows of the sun in different places.

They had their knowledge of mathematics, and a few crude tools: peepholes, sundials, measuring rods, compasses for drawing circles. They had a water clock and a sun stick, with the length of its shadow marked off into twelve parts which showed, roughly, the hours of the day. Of course, these hours of daylight were fewer in winter and more in summer.

Notwithstanding, the astronomers at the Museum, and later the students they taught, added much to the world's knowledge of astronomy.

They charted the course of the sun's annual path among the stars. By their observations of the time when certain bright stars appeared on the horizon, they estimated the seasons and the length of the year. At Alexandria they made a catalog of all the visible stars, and mapped their positions.

What we now call the solar system, astronomers

at that time called the universe, and they thought the earth was its center. How could they know, as we know today, that the earth is just a tiny speck in the universe, millions of times smaller, in comparison, than a speck of dust is to the earth?

Most astronomers thought the universe looked like this,

They thought the earth stood still, at the center of the great, revolving globe of the heavens, to which the stars were fixed.

with the sun revolving around the earth.

They thought that most of the stars were "fixed," fastened somehow in place against the sky. But what about those stars that seemed to move? The Greeks called them *planets,* which meant "wanderers." Since the astronomers had only their own eyes to see with, they found only five planets, but they noticed many things about them.

The smallest and fastest one, they called Mercury, for the messenger of the gods.

They called the brightest one Venus, for the goddess of beauty.

Mars, shining red, they named after the god of war.

Jupiter, because it was so big, got its name from the king of the gods. And the one that seemed to move very slowly they called Saturn, after the god who sometimes could make time stand still.

The Roman writer, Macrobius, said that Archimedes estimated the distances to the five planets.

Aristarchus, who taught astronomy at the Museum, pictured the universe as much larger than the other astronomers did, and he boldly said that although the earth was the center of the universe it was not fixed, but traveled around the sun in a great circle.

In many things Archimedes agreed with Aristarchus, but he thought that the universe was even bigger — much bigger. Nobody had ever said that the stars were so far away. Today we know that even the distances inside the solar system are greater than what Archimedes thought was the distance to the farthest star.

Archimedes thought that the earth revolved in a sphere around the sun, within another sphere of the fixed stars.

Archimedes built an instrument for measuring the angles of the rising sun.

Archimedes disagreed with other astronomers on the size of the earth, too, but he thought it was larger than it actually is. His friend Eratosthenes, using a combination of astronomical observation and geometry, correctly estimated the circumference of the earth to within one hundred miles. Eratosthenes said the distance around the earth was 300,000 *stadia,* which is almost exactly right. Archimedes said the perimeter of the earth was 3,000,000 *stadia.*

Because it was the most important thing in the sky, the Greeks thought a great deal about the sun, and its size.

Anaxagorus, the first Greek to say that the sun was red-hot, and bigger than the mainland of Greece, was banished forever. But now, in Archimedes' time, astronomers knew that it was bigger than the moon and even bigger than the earth. But how big?

The astronomer Eudoxus said that the sun was nine times greater than the moon.

Phidias, Archimedes' father, said that it was twelve times larger.

Aristarchus said that the sun was almost twenty times larger. And Archimedes calmly said that they were all wrong, that the sun was at least thirty times larger than the moon. (Do you know how much larger the sun actually is? About 1,320,000 times larger.)

Archimedes spent a lot of time trying to calculate the exact length of the year. The Greek calendar was a mess, because although it divided the year into twelve months, the months were based on the phases of the moon, instead of on the time it took the earth to travel around the sun. The Greek year had 354 days, so things got all mixed up.

The year began with the first new moon after the summer solstice — the longest day of the year. Each month was 28 days long, from new moon to new moon, so that there were always days left over when the next solstice came around. Some months therefore were given 29 days, and some 30 — and every eight years an extra three months were added to the year!

Even this complicated system didn't work. The calendar got so mixed up that the festivals were always happening at the wrong time of the year. It was certainly confusing to have the spring festival in the middle of winter, or the harvest festival in the early spring.

We are pretty sure that Archimedes estimated the length of the year accurately, because of the precision of his astronomical machine.

The machine is described in one of Archimedes' lost works, called *On Sphere Making*. It is also described by the Roman, Cicero, who saw it when he visited Sicily many years after Archimedes died. After the capture of Sicily, the Roman general, Marcellus, took some of Archimedes' astronomical machines back to Rome, where they were carefully preserved for more than two hundred years.

Archimedes built the machines to demonstrate the Eudoxian system of the universe. Eudoxus was a Greek mathematician and astronomer, the first to explain the movements of the planets in a scientific manner.

(Do you know what held the other astronomers back? Until they realized that the earth, too, was moving around the sun, and that they were seeing the planets from a kind of moving platform, they could find no pattern at all in the planets' paths.)

We all know what *concentric circles* are. They are circles one inside another, with a common center.

Concentric circles have a common center.

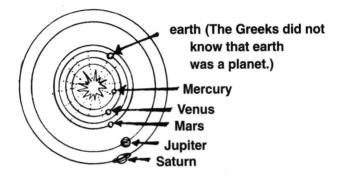

Eudoxus said that the universe was made of a series of concentric spheres, each sphere supporting a planet in its path.

Archimedes' astronomical machine was made of glass spheres, one inside another, which were turned by water power. The spheres that held the sun, the moon, and the planets rotated so accurately that the machine even showed the periods of the moon and the eclipses of the sun and moon.

Archimedes' astronomical machine illustrated the relative positions and motions of all the bodies in the solar system that were then known. It was actually the first planetarium.

Archimedes never lost his interest in astronomy. He realized that its study was a way of applying his beloved mathematics to nature. Like his fellow Greeks, he believed that astronomy was geometry in motion.

Later, he combined his knowledge of the paths of the sun's rays with his discoveries in geometry to build a device that set fire to the Roman ships during the siege of Syracuse.

Many of Archimedes' investigations in geometry, though he did not think they had any practical importance, have been useful to astronomers ever since. He could never know that some of the curves he worked with —
the *parabola*,

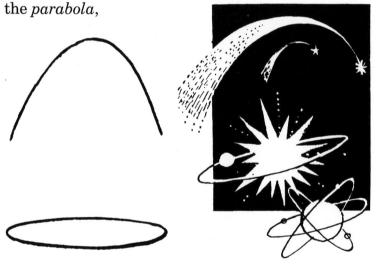

and the *ellipse* —
are the paths taken by all bodies controlled by the laws of gravity.

As you will see later, Archimedes had some ideas of his own about gravity, without ever knowing what it was.

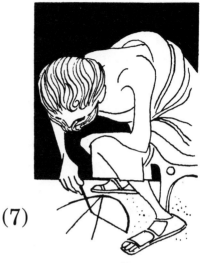

(7)

Archimedes and Mathematics

THE WORD "mathematics" comes from the Greek word, *mathema,* which means "science."

Mathematics was the thing Archimedes liked best, and he worked in every kind of mathematics known to the ancient world. He did not, like Euclid, write textbooks for the use of mathematics students. Archimedes wrote brilliant, complicated essays, to be read and studied by the most advanced mathematicians of his time, his friends at Alexandria.

He worked with arithmetic, which studies numbers. All mathematicians need numbers. Everybody needs numbers.

He worked in trigonometry, which relates distances to directions. Engineers need trigonometry and so do astronomers, navigators, and surveyors.

He laid the groundwork for the development of the calculus, which deals with motion and change. There could be no rockets, no space travel, without the calculus.

Archimedes particularly loved geometry, which is the study of shapes in space: flat shapes, drawn on paper (or sand), and solid shapes that take up room in the world.

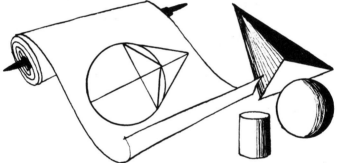

Architects couldn't plan buildings without geometry. Surveyors couldn't make maps. Nobody could design an airplane, a boat, or a rocket. Engineers couldn't build bridges. Artists need it for drawing pictures; plumbers need it for putting in pipes. Navigators need geometry, and so do physicists.

Archimedes carried the study of geometry farther than any other man in ancient times, and he made many important discoveries about solids:

about spheres, like the earth or the moon or a ball or a balloon;

about cylinders, like a glass or a pipe or a log; about cubes, like a box;

and about cones, like a mountain or a pine tree or an ice cream cone.

He studied their relationships to each other and to flat surfaces.

He studied circles
and semicircles,
triangles
and angles,
straight lines and curved lines,
spirals,
hyperbolas,
parabolas
and ellipses.

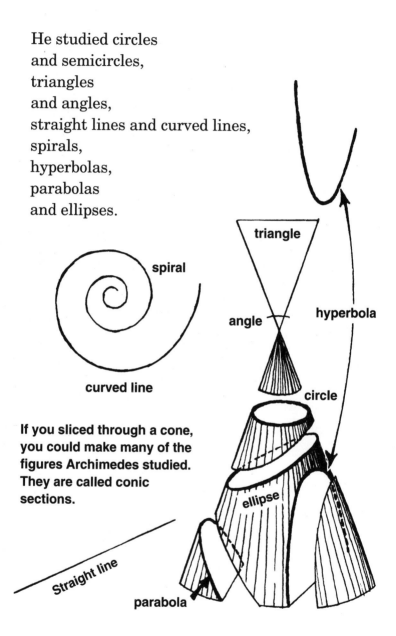

spiral

curved line

triangle

angle

hyperbola

circle

If you sliced through a cone, you could make many of the figures Archimedes studied. They are called conic sections.

Straight line

ellipse

parabola

84

To find the volume of this box, you multiply the length × the width × the height.

Archimedes discovered how to find the volume, which is the space or material contained, of many solid figures. Because of his work on the volume of spheres, scientists who came after him could figure out such things as the weight of the sun and the moon and the earth; how much space there is in the solar system; how much gas it takes to fill a balloon.

Because we can find the volume of a cylinder, we know how much oil a pipeline will carry, how much wood there is in a tree, how big to make the fuel tanks of a rocket.

All of our modern measurements of solids started with Archimedes.

All of our modern measurements of curvilinear surfaces — surfaces bounded by curved lines, like circles or ellipses — started with Archimedes, too.

Archimedes developed what we now call "higher mathematics." Many of the advanced and difficult problems he worked out were lost for hundreds of years and only rediscovered in modern times.

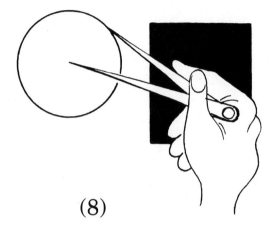

(8)

The Measurement of a Circle

Do YOU know what this is? π

It is the Greek letter called *pi*.

You will use it many times in mathematics when you are working with circles. If you want to find the area of a circle,

you multiply pi

times the radius of the circle — which is the length of a line from the center of the circle to its rim, or circumference,

times the radius again. (When you multiply anything by itself, you square it.)

The formula that always gives you the area of a circle looks like this.

$a = \pi r^2$ (area = pi times the radius of the circle, squared)

But what is pi?

What number does it stand for?

Pi = 3.14159.

This is how you would work the problem of the circle's area.

If you have a circle like this, with a radius of 2 inches,

radius

you could find its area by first multiplying 2×2, and then multiplying 4×3.14159.

Did you get 12.56636 square inches for the answer? That is the area of the circle.

How would you find the area of a circle with a radius of 3 inches?

First, multiply 3 × 3. That is 9. Then multiply 9 × 3.14159.

The area of a 3-inch circle is 28.27431 square inches.

But if you were trying to figure out the area of a circle, and you did not know the formula, $a = \pi r^2$, how would you do it?

Archimedes devised a way.

Long before, people had discovered how to find the area of a rectangle by multiplying its length by its width.

And they discovered that you could find the *approximate* area of a circle by drawing the largest possible square inside the circle, and the smallest possible square outside the circle, like this.

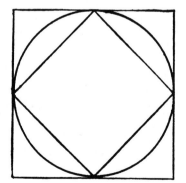

Then if you found the area of the inside square, and the area of the outside square, you would know that the area of the circle was something between those numbers.

In this way, you could also find the approximate circumference of the circle, the distance around the edge. It has to be something between the perimeter, or distance around the edge, of the larger square and the smaller one.

But Archimedes wanted to be more exact. Instead of enclosing his circle in two squares, he enclosed it in two *polygons* (polygons are many-sided figures). You can see right away that the sizes of the polygons are much closer to the size of the circle than the squares are — and these polygons have only eight sides.

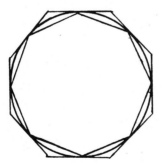

Archimedes added more and more sides until he had two polygons of 96 sides each. Then the two polygons and the circle between them were right on top of each other.

Now he proved that the circumference he found with his 96-sided polygons was always less than $3\frac{1}{7}$ times the distance across the circle (its *diameter*) and always more than $3\frac{10}{71}$ times the diameter. That's what pi is. It is the ratio — or the way the two always compare — between the circumference of a circle and its diameter.

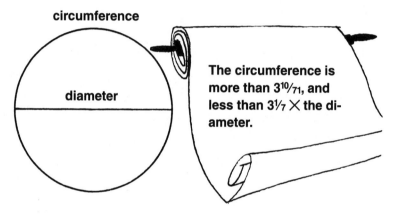

circumference

diameter

The circumference is more than $3\frac{10}{71}$, and less than $3\frac{1}{7}$ × the diameter.

Archimedes had already proved that the area of a circle was the same as the area of a right triangle, like this,

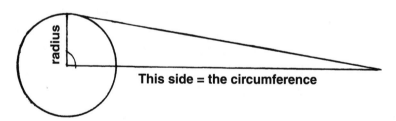

radius

This side = the circumference

if one side of the right angle was the same as the radius of the circle,
and the other side was the same as the circumference.
And now he had a quick way to find the circumference.

Finally he proved that the ratio (the way the two always compare) of the area of a circle, to the diameter of that circle, squared, is always 11 to 14.

The figure for pi that we use today is 3.14159. (You can carry this number to as many decimal places as you want. It will never come out even.) Archimedes lived long before the decimal system was invented, but his figure for pi would have been between 3.1408 and 3.1428, which was pretty accurate! Pi is sometimes called the "Archimedean number."

One thing that has always interested mathematicians who have studied Archimedes' work, is that he showed, in his writing on *The Measurement of a Circle*, that he had some way of finding the square roots of numbers, a discovery that was supposed to have come later.

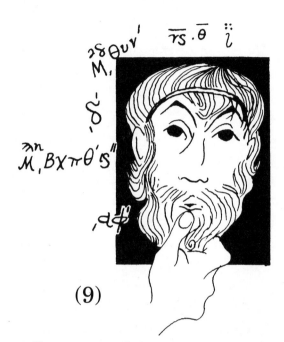

(9)

Archimedes and Numbers

ARCHIMEDES wrote two papers on arithmetic. One was on the principles of numeration — or counting — and is now lost.

The Greek system of numeration was fairly new. Probably it had been introduced by the mathematicians at Alexandria. It was a clumsy system, but with it the Greeks managed to do all the things they needed numbers for. In the papers he wrote, Archimedes used this Greek system of numeration, but some mathematicians think that between themselves, Archimedes and Apollonius used some kind of decimal system. They think that the lost paper might have explained this system.

The other paper on arithmetic was called *The Sand Reckoner.*

In *The Sand Reckoner*, Archimedes set out to prove that there was a practical way of working with really big numbers. He said that there were numbers bigger than all the grains of sand in Sicily — bigger, even, than the number of grains of sand it would take to fill the universe.

He said that there was *nothing* you couldn't measure with numbers and still have numbers left over. He said that there was no end to numbers.

No end to numbers? That seemed impossible!

Why, everyone (or almost everyone) knew that even the number of grains of sand on all the beaches of Sicily was infinite, or "without end." But Archimedes proved that you could number them all, and still have numbers left over.

Archimedes started his calculations with the biggest number the Greeks had a name for, the *myriad*. A myriad was 10,000. Multiplying it by itself, he got a myriad myriad, which was 100,000,000.

Then he showed that you could multiply that number by itself, or square it, and reach a number that was 100,000,000 multiplied by itself 100,000,000 times. But it was still a number, wasn't it?

Then Archimedes showed that this was hardly a beginning of numbers. He went on until he reached a number he called $P^{100,000,000}$, which is so big that there would not be room in the universe as we know it today to write it out.

But there were more numbers still.

Then Archimedes estimated the number of grains of sand that would fill the universe.

He figured first in *grains*, then in *poppy seed*, which were a common Greek measure. Then he went on to *fingerbreadths*, which were 40 times longer than poppy seeds, and then to *stadia*, which were 10,000 fingerbreadths. (A *stadium* was a Greek measure 600 feet long.)

Up and up went Archimedes in his figuring, filling first the sphere of the earth with grains of sand, then the Greek universe (our solar system), which he said was 10,000 times greater than the earth, then the sphere of the fixed stars, which he said was 10,000 times greater than the universe.

And still, he had only come to a number which we would write like this: 10^{63}, or ten to the sixty-third power.

There are more numbers than there are grains of sand, or anything else, in the universe, even as we know it. Modern scientists work with these immense numbers every day. Computers have to do the mathematics for them because there would not be time in a man's life to work out some of the answers.

But even a computer could never come to the end of numbers. As Archimedes showed, there is no end to numbers.

Numbers are infinite.

For fun, Archimedes sent a problem for the mathematicians of Alexandria to work out. It is known as "the cattle problem," and here it is, though you should know algebra to work it out. (It must have been even harder for the Greeks, because they didn't have algebra.)

The sun had a herd of bulls and cows.

Some were white, some were gray, some were brown, and some were spotted.

The number of spotted bulls was less than the number of white bulls by 5/6 of the number of gray bulls.

It was less than the number of gray bulls by 9/20 of the number of brown bulls.

It was less than the number of brown bulls by 13/42 of the number of white bulls.

The number of white cows was $\frac{7}{12}$ of the number of all the gray cows and bulls together.

The number of gray cows was $\frac{9}{20}$ of the number of brown cows and bulls.

The number of brown cows was $\frac{11}{30}$ of the number of spotted cows and bulls.

The number of spotted cows was $\frac{13}{42}$ of the number of white cows and bulls.

Archimedes challenged his friends to find how many of each color of cattle were in the sun's herd.

The answer is indeterminate, or in other words there can be a number of right answers. But the lowest possible number of each would be:

spotted bulls	4,149,387	spotted cows	5,439,213
white bulls	10,366,482	white cows	7,206,360
brown bulls	7,358,060	brown cows	3,515,820
gray bulls	7,460,514	gray cows	4,893,246

In Archimedes' own solution to the puzzle, each of these numbers was 80 times larger than that given here.

Some people think that Archimedes might not have made this puzzle at all, because it was written in verse, and he was not known as a poet. But most mathematicians think that it was his, and that it might have been put into verse by someone who copied it later.

Another Greek, to make the problem even more interesting, said that some of the answers had to be in square numbers and some had to be in triangular numbers.

The Greeks loved to play with numbers by shape, both for fun and for the things they learned this way.

This is a square number.

This is a triangular number.

What can you tell about square numbers from these?

What can you tell about triangular numbers from these?

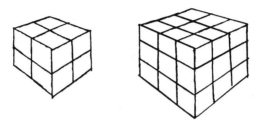

What can you tell about cube numbers from these?

Square numbers

Could you see that the number on any one side is the same as the number on any other side?

Could you see that if you multiply the number on any side by itself, that gives you the number of things in the square?

Triangular numbers

Could you see that to get the next triangular number you add a bottom line one thing bigger than the last triangular number?

Did you find the pattern in the way the triangle numbers jumped?

(3 + 3 = 6, 6 + 4 = 10, 10 + 5 = 15 . . .)

Cube numbers

Could you see that you have to multiply three numbers to get a cube number? When you find the volume of something like a box you are using cube numbers, because you are multiplying *length × width × height.*

How many other numbers-by-shape can you think of?

(10)

Archimedes and the
Centers of Gravity

NOBODY is really sure what gravity is. We only know how it acts. We usually think that the first real understanding of the laws of gravitation began in the seventeenth century, with Sir Isaac Newton. But two thousand years before Newton, Greek scientists had the first glimmerings of the idea of gravity and the effect it had on everything on earth. They even suspected that everything they could see in the universe followed some similar law.

Archimedes was thinking and experimenting with equilibrium — or balance — and the centers of gravity of both solid things like the earth, and liquid things like water.

His demonstrations of centers of gravity were the foundation of the science of theoretical mechanics, or the theory of mechanics.

The center of gravity is the point where the whole weight of an object seems to center. Any object will balance at its center of gravity.

If you have ever carried a long board or a pair of skis over your shoulder, you know that there is a place on them where they balance. This place is their center of gravity.

If you stand on one foot, you can balance as long as your center of gravity is over that foot. If you lean over so far that your center of gravity is not over that foot, you will fall. The Leaning Tower of Pisa doesn't fall because its center of gravity is still over the base of the tower.

In Archimedes' books on mechanics he proved many things that he had discovered. He proved that the center of gravity is not always in the center of an object. If something has a heavy end and a light end, the center of gravity is closer to the heavy end.

Have you ever tried balancing a spoon on your finger?

Try it. Does it balance in the middle?

What can you tell about the weight of the spoon on this side of the balancing point,

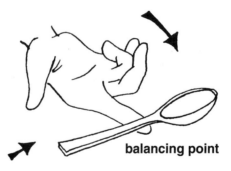

balancing point

and this side?

They must be equal.

Archimedes experimented with weights at equal distances.

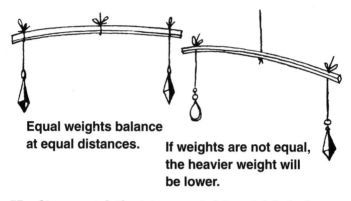

Equal weights balance at equal distances.

If weights are not equal, the heavier weight will be lower.

He discovered that two weights which balance at equal distances are equal.

But if the weights are unequal, the heavier weight will be lower. That is because gravity pulls harder on heavy things than on light ones.

If you took a piece of stiff wire and stuck a big gumdrop on one end and a little gumdrop on the other, the center of gravity would be much closer to the big gumdrop.

Now suppose the big gumdrop is the earth, and the little gumdrop is the moon.

Scientists have found out that the earth and the moon are so close together in space that the sun cannot pull on one without pulling on the other, any more than the earth's gravity could pull on only one of those gumdrops.

Do you think that the center of the earth is its center of gravity? No it isn't. The earth's center of gravity in the solar system is the balancing point between the weight of the earth and the weight of the moon — 20,000 miles from the moon.

One of the best ways to learn about centers of gravity is to make a mobile.

You need some sticks,

some thread,

and an assortment of smallish objects of different weights.

You can make the mobile as simple or as complicated as you wish, but each section of it has to balance, like this.

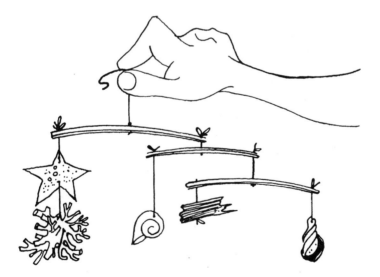

Don't forget to start from the bottom and work up.

103

Archimedes discovered methods for finding the centers of gravity of many kinds of plane figures —
triangles,
parallelograms,
parabolas,
and more.

You can, too, if you cut them out of cardboard and find their balancing points. If you use different colors, you can make a wonderful Archimedean mobile.

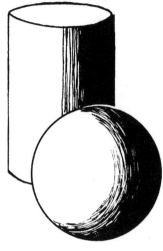

(11)

The Sphere and
the Cylinder

ARCHIMEDES considered his work with spheres and cylinders — and the many discoveries he made about them — to be the most important of his life. He wrote about the areas and the volumes of spheres,

and cylinders,

cones and pyramids,

and all plane and solid figures related to them.

Do you know the difference between a plane and a solid figure?

A plane figure is flat, like these,

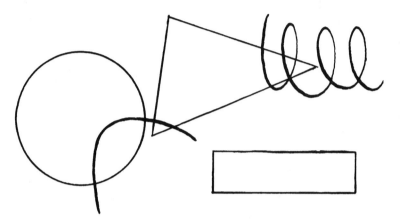

drawn on a page.

They have only *two dimensions:* length and width.

A solid figure has three dimensions: length, width, and thickness.

The sphere is the solid of a circle.

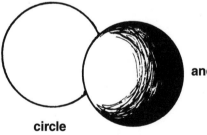

circle and sphere

The cone is the solid of a triangle.

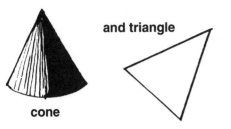

and triangle

**This tetrahedron
can be the solid
of a triangle, too**

cone

The box is the solid of a rectangle. The cube is the solid of a square.

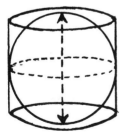

box

and rectangle

Of all Archimedes' discoveries, this was his favorite: if you took a sphere,
and made a cylinder whose base was the greatest circle of the sphere,

**The height is the
diameter of the sphere**

The base is the greatest circle of the sphere

and whose height was the diameter of the sphere,

107

the cylinder would take up 1½ times as much space as the sphere,

its volume would be 1½ times as much,

and if you measured the surfaces of the sphere and the cylinder, the surface of the cylinder would be 1½ times larger than the surface of the sphere.

Archimedes said that the ratio, or relationship, of the cylinder to the sphere was ³⁄₂.

He thought the discovery was so important that he wanted this figure placed on his tomb.

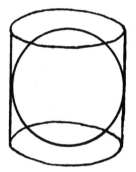

When Archimedes sent his two books on *The Sphere and the Cylinder* to Alexandria, he played a practical joke on his friends there, misstating some of his results to see if he could catch them napping. He said he did it to "deceive those vain geometricians who say they have found everything, but never give their proofs, and sometimes claim that they have discovered what is impossible."

Did the mathematicians of Alexandria catch him in his joke? Probably some of them did.

Archimedes' *Method,* the way he set his problems down and then proved them, has been very important to all the mathematicians who followed him. It gave them a logical way to start any problem, and an orderly way of setting things down, one by one, discarding false statements and proving true ones, until they had reached a conclusion.

Someone once said that his method was like the tactics of a master of strategy, who foresees everything, eliminates the unnecessary things, masters every position and every possibility, then, in conclusion, strikes the final blow.

When Archimedes, working by his method, wrote down the proofs, one by one, everything seemed so simple and logical that people could almost be convinced that *anyone* could have done it!

The War Machines of Archimedes

UNDER the reign of King Hiero, Syracuse was peaceful and prosperous. The city was spacious and beautiful, the markets were filled with goods, the docks and shipyards were crowded and bustling.

But all around Syracuse, in the Mediterranean, there was war. And there was always fighting between one and another of the city-states of Greece.

The fiercest struggle was between the two great powers of the Mediterranean: Rome and Carthage.

Carthage was a great city on the Mediterranean coast of Africa. She had colonies in Spain, and controlled almost all of Sicily except Syracuse. The ships of Carthage had mastery of all the western Mediterranean Sea. Any foreign vessels they caught sailing there were rammed and sunk. On land, Carthage was pushing steadily eastward, and taking over all of Sicily.

But Rome, too, was growing more and more powerful. One by one, her legions had captured the Greek city-states in Italy.

The Romans and the Carthaginians, trying to find a way to divide the Mediterranean between themselves, made an agreement. They decided that no Carthaginian ships should trade in the ports of Italy, and no Roman ships should enter the ports of Sicily.

111

If Carthage controlled the Strait of Messina, Rome could be cut off from her own ports in Eastern Italy.

Rome was angry at not being able to trade in Sicily.

But look at this map again.

It angered the Roman merchants to be so close to the busy, prosperous ports of Sicily and not to be allowed to trade there.

And the Carthaginians could see that if they cut off the Strait of Messina, they would cut off the Romans on the west coast of Italy from their own ports on the east coast. To get around the bottom of Italy, the Romans had either to sail through the Strait of Messina or go all the way around Sicily, into the Carthage-controlled western Mediterranean.

King Hiero knew that sooner or later Syracuse was going to be caught in the war between Rome and Carthage, and he was terribly worried. How could Syracuse defend herself? True, she had an alliance with Rome. But the Romans were fighting in so

112

many places! Would they be able to spare the men and ships to protect Syracuse against the mighty fleet of Carthage?

Many times, Hiero discussed the situation with Archimedes.

"See how we are situated," he said. "Here on this peninsula we can be cut off so completely that no help can come to us from our allies. Syracuse has been taken by siege before. I beg of you, Archimedes, help me make plans for defending the city."

Archimedes shook his head impatiently.

"I am becoming an old man," he said. "And there is still so much I have to do, so much I want to find out. I have no time to play at war like a boy, or with the toys of war. Besides, science is to me something to make men grow, not to destroy them."

But Hiero persisted for days and weeks and months. He would let Archimedes have no peace. At last he used the argument that had always worked.

"Think what you will be doing for the cause of science, Archimedes," he pleaded. "Think what it would mean if a man of science could provide the means to defend a city when the men of arms could not."

Finally Archimedes agreed. And once he started, his mind was crowded with ideas for machines to defend the city. He would use all he knew about mechanics. Whoever those future attackers were, if they ever came they would have some surprises.

He made drawing after drawing, and steadily the machines were built by the workmen of the king, then stored away.

Hiero commanded that Archimedes' machines were always to be kept in good working order. No ropes were to be allowed to fray, rotting wood must be replaced, no metal must rust. And there must always be men trained to use the machines.

"Even if they are not used for twenty years," he said, "or even for a lifetime, men must always be trained to use the machines. The time will come when Syracuse will need them."

Hiero was right. He never saw the time during his life, but in the year 215 B.C. Hiero died, and his grandson, Hieronymus, inherited the crown.

But Hieronymus did not hold power long. Hippocrates, a traitor who had been bribed by Carthage, murdered Hieronymus and seized control of the city.

Then Hippocrates broke the long alliance between Rome and Syracuse and made a new alliance with Carthage.

At once the Romans made war on Syracuse. They sent a fleet and army against the city under the command of Marcellus, one of the greatest of the Roman generals.

Marcellus not only was a Roman, who wanted to take Syracuse forever out of the hands of Carthage and make the Strait of Messina safe for Roman ships, but he was a bitter personal enemy of the treacherous Hippocrates.

Setting up his camp near the walls of the city, Marcellus prepared to attack Syracuse from the land and from the sea.

He had a great fleet of sixty towering galleys, each with six banks of oars. In his fleet was a huge war machine, built to cast stones and darts at the city. The machine was so big that it was supported on a bridge of planks placed across the decks of eight ships chained together.

When the people of Syracuse heard about the fleet and army of Marcellus they were terribly frightened, and they called upon Hippocrates to save them. Hippocrates was terrified. Where were his friends from Carthage, who had promised to come to his aid?

He certainly did not have enough trained soldiers to stand against Marcellus! Of course, he remembered, there were those men trained in the use of Archimedes' machines. He would have to use those men and the machines, although he did not understand them.

He had the uneasy feeling, too, that Archimedes held him in great contempt. Still, the man must love Syracuse, and he had the reputation of being a wizard of some sort. Hippocrates started to send for Archimedes, then changed his mind and went to him himself. He questioned him closely about the machines.

"You can depend on them," said Archimedes quietly. "I shall direct their use myself."

With his robes flapping and his beard blowing in the wind, Archimedes was everywhere about the city, placing the machines.

Here is the account of the battle as it was written by the great Roman historian, Plutarch:

When, therefore, the Romans assaulted the walls at two places at once, fear and consternation stupefied the Syracusans, believing that nothing was able to resist that violence and those forces. But when Archimedes began to ply his engines, he at once shot against the land forces all sorts of missile weapons, and immense masses of stones that came down with incredible noise and violence; against which no man could stand, for they knocked down those upon whom they fell in heaps, breaking all their ranks and files.

In the meantime, huge poles thrust out from the walls over the ships, sank some by the great weights which they let down from on high upon them; others they lifted up into the air by an iron hand or beak like a crane's beak, and when they had drawn them up by the prow, and set them on end upon the poop, they plunged them to the bottom of the sea; or else the ships, drawn by engines within, and whirled about, were dashed against steep rocks that stood jutting out under the walls, with great destruction of the soldiers who were aboard them.

A ship was frequently lifted up to a great height in the air (a dreadful thing to behold) and was rolled to

and fro, and kept swinging, until the mariners were all thrown out, when at length it was dashed against the rocks or let fall. At the engine which Marcellus brought upon the bridge of ships, which was called *Sambuca,* from some resemblance it had to an instrument of music, while it was as yet approaching the wall, there was discharged a piece of rock of ten talents weight, then a second and a third, which, striking upon it with an immense force and a noise like thunder, broke all its foundation to pieces, shook out all its fastenings, and completely dislodged it from the bridge. So Marcellus, doubtful what counsel to pursue, drew off his ships to a safer distance and sounded a retreat to his forces on land.

They then took a resolution of coming up under the walls, if it were possible, in the night; thinking that as Archimedes used ropes stretched at length in playing his engines, the soldiers would now be under the shot, and the darts would, for want of sufficient distance to throw them, fly over their heads without effect.

But Archimedes, it appeared, had long before framed for such occasions engines accommodated to any distance, and shorter weapons; and had made numerous small openings in the walls through which, with engines of a shorter range, unexpected blows were inflicted on the assailants. Thus, when they who thought to deceive the defenders came close up to the walls, instantly a shower of darts and other missile weapons was again cast upon them. And when stones came tumbling down perpendicularly upon their heads, and, as it were, the whole wall shot out arrows at them, they retired.

And now again, as they were going off, arrows and darts of a longer range inflicted a great slaughter among them, and their ships were driven one against another; while they themselves were not able to retaliate in any way. For Archimedes had provided and fixed most of his engines immediately under the wall; whence the Romans, seeing that mischief overwhelmed them from no visible means, began to think they were fighting with the gods.

120

Yet Marcellus escaped unhurt, and deriding his own artificers and engineers, "What," said he, "must we give up fighting with this geometrical Briareus, who plays pitch-and-toss with our ships, and, with the multitude of darts which he showers at a single moment upon us, really outdoes the hundred-handed giants of mythology?" And doubtless the rest of the Syracusans were but the body of Archimedes' designs, one soul moving and governing all; for, laying aside all other arms, with this alone they infested the Romans and protected themselves. In fine, when such terror had seized upon the Romans, that, if they did but see a little rope or a piece of wood from the wall, instantly crying out that there it was

again, Archimedes was about to let fly some engine at them, they turned their backs and fled, Marcellus desisted from conflicts and assaults, putting all his hopes in a long siege.

Did you wonder how Marcellus knew who was responsible for the machines? All educated men knew Archimedes of Syracuse and this could be the work of no other hand!

One later account of this battle says that Archimedes also placed on the wall huge concave mirrors made of highly polished metal. He had designed the mirrors as parabolas which caught and focused the rays of the sun so accurately (some of our modern lenses work the same way) that when these rays were beamed at any of the wooden ships in Marcellus' fleet for a short time, the ship caught fire.

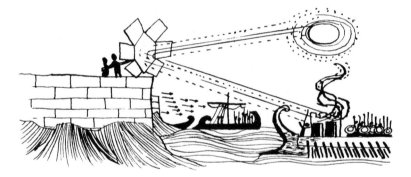

Historians are not sure whether these burning mirrors were actually a part of Archimedes' defense of Syracuse, as they were not mentioned in any immediate accounts of the battle, as the other war machines were. But the machine was later described in detail, and almost nine hundred years afterward a French scientist, Buffon, made a mirror following the description and succeeded in setting fire to wood 150 feet away, and melting lead at a distance of 140 feet.

During the battle, Archimedes was everywhere at once. No longer did he think of his machines as toys, but as giant working models of geometry and mechanics. He had used levers and pulleys, cranks, screws, and cogwheels. He had used not only man power to work the machines, but air power and water power. He had used the knowledge he had of balance and centers of gravity. He had used the things he knew about different kinds of curves, and about applying forces over distances.

And how Archimedes enjoyed his practical geometry lesson! He was only sorry that King Hiero was not there to see it.

He often walked along the walls where the machines stood ready, waiting for Marcellus to return with his fleet and legions. But Marcellus was a wise general. He had given up the idea of capturing Syracuse by attack, and instead, blockaded the city by land and sea.

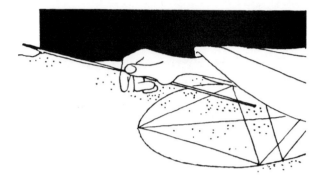

(13)

The End of Archimedes

FOR THREE YEARS Marcellus held Syracuse in siege, but he did not just sit outside the walls and wait. He overran a great part of Sicily and won many towns from the Carthaginians. He captured the camp of Hippocrates and killed him and eight thousand of his men.

He watched Syracuse and waited. He explored and he planned.

One day in 212 B.C. he noticed a wall and a tower that were poorly guarded, and he had his workmen build scaling ladders to their measure.

124

The people of Syracuse were sure that the machines of Archimedes would protect them forever, and so they had grown very careless. True, there were some supply shortages, but otherwise they had almost forgotten they were at war.

The Feast to Diana was a festival the Syracusans loved, and they celebrated it with dancing and games, with food and wine. They celebrated so merrily that the Roman soldiers crept over the wall and into many parts of the city without ever being noticed.

At daybreak Marcellus ordered his soldiers everywhere to sound their trumpets. The blare of the trumpets from many directions, the sight of the Roman soldiers appearing in the streets, the noise of their running feet, and the clang of their armor started a panic in the city. Believing they had already been conquered, the people of Syracuse fled screaming in all directions.

Marcellus watched from the hill, with tears streaming down his face. The city was beautiful, and he knew that in a few hours it would be plundered, blackened and burning, with many of its people dead. Plundering was considered the right of soldiers, and no officer, not even Marcellus, dared forbid it.

But he ordered all his men to take as slaves only those who were slaves already, and to leave the citizens of Syracuse free.

"And above all," Marcellus commanded his men, "let no one dare lay hand on the person of Archimedes, or on his house or his belongings. I long to meet this man, to sit down and talk with him, and to pay honor to a mind that dwarfs the thinking of most men.

"When you reach the house of Archimedes, bring him instantly before me."

In his house, Archimedes was working on a problem. He sat bent over a diagram he had drawn in the sand on the floor. He was so intent on it that he had forgotten the war. He did not hear the shouts, the screaming, or the trumpets, or smell the smoke, or know the city had been taken.

His mind and his eyes were on his problem, and when a Roman soldier appeared and spoke to him, he heard his voice as if from a long way off.

"I command you, old man," the soldier shouted roughly, "to follow me instantly to the general, Marcellus."

Archimedes hardly glanced at him. "Leave me, leave me," he said impatiently. "Can't you see that I am working? I must finish my problem, and only then will I come to your Marcellus. The problem is more important, so go away! How can I leave this, unanswered and imperfect?"

The soldier laughed, and put his foot squarely on the drawing.

"Stand off my diagram, you are spoiling it!" Archimedes cried angrily. "Stand off, I say!" And he brought his drawing stick down sharply on the soldier's sandal.

The soldier stepped back, white with fury. Drawing his sword he ran Archimedes through, as the old man was bending again to his problem.

When Marcellus heard that Archimedes was dead he had the soldier killed as a common murderer, and mourned Archimedes as a friend. He sought out the old man's friends and relatives and honored them, and he had Archimedes buried with great ceremony.

And on his tomb he had engraved this figure.

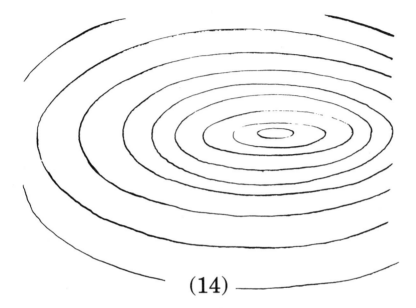

No End to Archimedes

DID YOU EVER drop a pebble in a pond, and watch the ripples spread out and out until they filled the pond?

Did you ever whisper in a cave, and hear the sound spread out and out until it filled the cave?

Did you know that a giant radio telescope can broadcast signals that spread out and out to fill millions of light-years of space?

Do you know what a chain reaction is, in a nuclear explosion? A single particle of an atom, billions of times smaller than anything you have ever seen, can set other atoms to exploding, each hitting others in a gigantic burst of power.

Some people's minds are like that. The things they think and the ideas they have and the discoveries they make never stop triggering other people's minds and other ideas, until the world is filled with them.

Archimedes' mind was like that: like a pebble in a pond, or a whisper in a cave, or the particle that starts a burst of power.

He began the science of mechanics
and the science of hydrostatics.
He discovered the principle of buoyancy,
and the principle of specific gravity,
the laws of the lever and pulleys,
and how to measure a circle.

He gave mathematicians a way of working, and was one of the first to apply scientific thinking to everyday problems.

Some people say he was the greatest mathematician of all time.

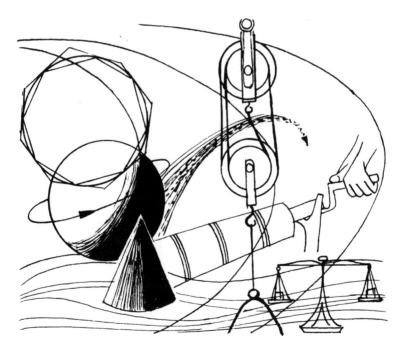

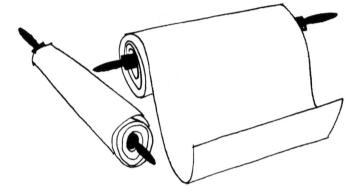

(Appendix)

Archimedes' Writings

HERE is a list of the writings of Archimedes, as far as anyone knows them. Some are lost; we know about them only because he refers to them in other writings, or because other mathematicians and historians of his time mention them. There may be still others that we don't know about at all, but that may be rediscovered in the translation of ancient manuscripts.

Some of these we have talked about.

Some are so complicated that they are only for advanced mathematicians, but you may want to study them someday.

The Measurement of a Circle

The Quadrature of the Parabola

A parabola looks like this,

and some of Archimedes' drawings for this book look like this.

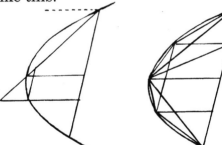

Spirals

The spiral of Archimedes looks like this.

The spiral of Archimedes has unusual mathematical properties which we use today in our calculations of speeds, directions, and distances in space.

Book of Lemmas

A *lemma* is an assumption or a premise taken for granted.

1 + 1 = 2 is a lemma.

Nobody expects you to stop and prove it.

But Archimedes' lemmas are much more complicated.

**A drawing from
The Book of Lemmas**

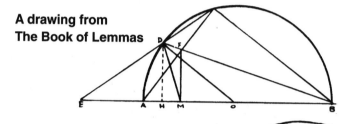

The Sphere and the Cylinder

Conoids and Spheroids

The Sand Reckoner

The Cattle Problem

Mechanics
Hydrostatics
On Floating Bodies
The Method of Treating Mechanical Problems

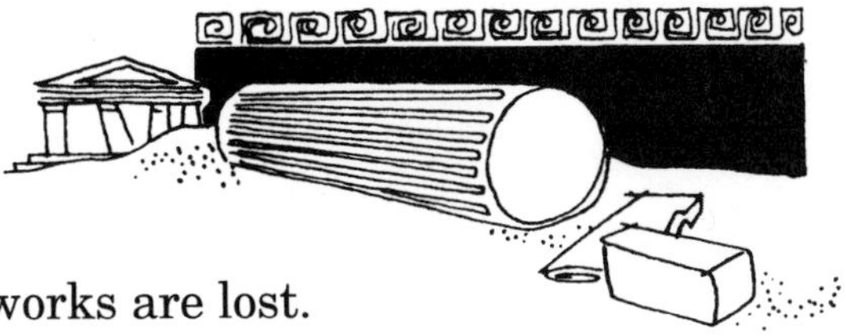

These works are lost.
The Principles of Numeration
On Levers
On Sphere Making
Semi-Regular Polyhedrons
Geometrical Methods
Parallel Lines
Triangles
The Properties of Right-Angled Triangles
Data
The Heptagon Inscribed in a Circle
Systems of Circles Touching One Another

Index

Author Profile

JEANNE BENDICK, a graduate of Parsons School of Design, is the author and illustrator of many books, primarily in the field of science. Her work has always been distinguished by her remarkable ability to express complex concepts in simple language, and to make difficult subjects interesting and comprehensible to the general reader. Among her many books are *The First Book of Space Travel*, *The First Book of Automobiles*, and *The First Book of Airplanes*.